Praise for IMPRESSIONS

"With its focus on a variety of topics, from music and the arts to poetic metaphors of life experience and growth, Impressions is an item of choice for a variety of readers. It will reach literature enthusiasts and philosophy students as well as those who look for beautiful expressions that use the mechanism of language to translate the thoughts and experiences of life into a meaningful draw that illustrates both the "power of the pen" and the ability to assemble "worthy thoughts" that lend to discussion and life celebration alike."

— D. Donovan, Senior Reviewer, Midwest Book Review

". . . Whether read in short or long doses, though, the writing is rhythmic, melodic, lyrical: "poetry mends the rift, while music bridges the gulf," Pandit notes, drawing on both. Sometimes, Pandit addresses an audience directly . . . —and in doing so gains the investment of thoughtful, patient readers invested in *style* and *ideas*. Upon reaching the end, any lingering doubts of the literary ambition of this work will have retreated.

In distinct style, *Impressions* considers the small yet profound daily experiences many of us tend to dismiss."

— booklife REVIEWS

". . . Pandit combines his training and profession in science with a passion for art and philosophy, right and left brain joined with heart, all connected to eyes that see the world with exquisite clarity."

— Larry W. Moore, Publisher, Broadstone Books

IMPRESSIONS

Short Letters by AMEYA PANDIT

IMPRESSIONS
Copyright © 2021 by Ameya D. Pandit

All rights reserved. No part of this work may be reproduced in any form or by any electronic or mechanical means, including information storage and retrieval systems, without written permission from the author, except for the use of brief quotations in a book review.

Requests for permission should be addressed to:

Ameya Dilip Pandit
ameya.pandit@gmail.com

FIRST EDITION

Edited by P. Tompkins
Designed by Euan Monaghan

ISBN: 978-1-7371045-0-6

Library of Congress Control Number: 2021909697

To

My children,
My wife,
My parents,
My sister,
My well-wishers,

... and to the unwavering
resolve of the human race

CONTENTS

Preface ix
On Childhood...............1
On Nature 51
On Arts........................97

PREFACE

This book is a culmination of my thoughts laid out over the course of many years. Some have been validated by my own experiences while others haven't. The material in these notes is nothing new—it lives in plain sight, within our grasp yet we seldom reflect on it. My attempt has been to present it in a form that I say is my own. Like every writer who searches for meaning so have I; without a meaning the writing feels meaningless; the few books I hold dear guide me in some way; the gifted souls I live with give me that push; I have taken their inspiration but I have imagined myself; this imagination is my own, and every chapter that follows is a flow of this imagination. If I have overstepped in this indulgence so as to suggest something else, it must be because of my necessity—a bold but a sincere one. I ask you to read the way you must, and if it makes you wonder, think, and perhaps change, the book has served its purpose. For no one can convince the other in entirety, and no one should. In the end, each is to his own. I have been asked who shall benefit from a read of such a book, and

I say to them, anyone; anyone who wishes to introspect, reflect, aspire, or dwell, be an artist, a poet, a scientist, or a composer—in essence every seeker of knowledge. The material I present is not time bound, so if this book does not find its audience today, it shall lie in wait for a readership tomorrow. Such is my quest. With that said, I leave you in the company of these pages with the hope that they may serve you the way they have served me. The Greek philosopher Seneca said, "Your thoughts or Your children." I only add—I have had the privilege of serving both.

Sincerely,
Pandit Ameya D.
August 22, 2020

INTRODUCTION TO CHAPTER 1

A blank page. A clean slate—the beginning of something. There is hope in such a thing, ask a writer, or an artist, of what a blank page brings, there is not much to show but there is plenty to imagine; there is excitement, energy, in the commencement of such a thing, or perhaps there is just the opposite—trepidation, fear, anxiety rule. This beginning is daunting, but it is a beginning nevertheless, signals an expression, an aspiration of something bigger, brighter—an idea. A birth of a child is also like this, another beginning—an idea, and might I add, a *formidable* one. This is the childhood I speak of, *those early years*, perhaps the most delicate and divine years of life. I leave the reader to decide when these years turn over, for every child is different, has his own curve, her own speed. I do not write to narrate the cuteness or the loveliness thereof, which nonetheless remains joyous and heartfelt, but I seek to explore and emphasize its brilliance—the commonality, the purity, and the objectivity. This for me is physics in action, mathematics at play, and art in illustration—a combination that yields a spectacle, a spectacle perhaps only nature can create. And rightfully so—this is her creation, her own work, made by her own material, obeying her own laws. We may replicate this creation in the labs of science, but then we merely imitate and set in motion the laws that are her very own. So for me this remains a work of hers, her original, just like her every other, a marvel perhaps, a marvel that needs to be seen, to be felt. I have felt this marvel in the thoughts that follow; I owe these to my children, to my indulgence with them, in their day, or their night, sometimes as an active actor, other times as a passive bystander. These thoughts are mine, but the material in them is not, *it belongs to every child*, to that phase of life, which rejoices the heart and satisfies the soul. It's a phase that vanishes well before our memories grow to seize and store; it's short lived but remains astonishingly heroic, amazingly resilient, yet nourishingly simple; it transcends every faith, every religion, and even unites everyone—or at least stands a chance. The world does not find anything new in the occurrence as such, it is abundantly common for any mention, yet it breathes a class of genius, a touch of magnificence—one this world fails to notice in its rush to line up the new and the fashionable. Like every marvel of nature that stands in front of our eyes, so does this— with its purity and objectivity. This is my aim, to narrate this phase, to capture its magnificence, to illustrate its brilliance, to highlight its substance, so as to give childhood what it thoroughly deserves—*its rightful due.*

CHAPTER 1

On Childhood

Babbles, those first words—are one of a kind. They delight the ear of a parent, are versatile in their form, impress the mind with their range and dimension. Every word spoken at this age has an expression—a show of a curious mind laden in spirit and action. A language is born, a discovery is made; from the depths of his[1] heart he speaks, he narrates the world and everything new his eyes see, and even if this prose may be imperfect to the head, it remains perfect for the soul.

§

The smile of a little child is the smile of life; he knows how to cry, but he learns when to smile, and while his cry sig-

---

[1] No gender preference . . . I have referred to a child as he and to nature as she

nals his own arrival, his smile illustrates a sweetness of all; both the cry and the smile manifest vigorously in his early years, he is fluent in both, a master in each; through them he narrates every emotion—even the world pauses to watch his act, and why not, for life is in action, as she speaks, of her secret, of how she remains wrapped up in the persuasive cry or the heartfelt smile.

§

I hear an anthem, I see the march of the troops, there is a show of strength, of stature; this is the anthem of a nation, a nation celebrating the continuance of a new era, the birth of its freedom; then after a while as the celebrations wind down, I hear a cry, a cry of a new life, one who may be a few months old; this I say is also an anthem, perhaps a far superior one, one that our ears invariably tune in to; one that needs no salute, no flag, no armor; one that lives in all yet unique to each, and one that a child speaks well before he knows his nation or his God; even the brave soldier lends his hand to protect such a one, for this anthem transcends every other, this is the anthem of life, the anthem of *our* humanity.

§

A big brother and his little sister—what a combination, a kinship in action. The little sister grabs her brother's hand—the brother obliges to her wish. To her tiny figure, her brother is a mountain to climb, an object of play, a specimen to grab. She leaps at him, pulls his hair, and even spoils his work—yet he does nothing, giving in, agreeing, obeying her every demand, resigning to her will, the will of a queen. To her little soul he offers a cushion of comfort, a mate who can play, a guardian who can protect. He is like the third parent, yet without the burden of being so; what it must be like to be in his shoes I wonder—he is a boy marching towards his manhood, yet whenever she grabs his hand he goes back a little; she does what none of us can do, she shows what we long to see, she brings out in him his long lost play; the innocence is seen, the loveliness felt; even time yields to her demand when she reveals her powers, holding back for him what he is sure to leave behind—his very own, the adorable childhood.

§

A child of a year in age expresses every emotion so cleanly; he does not conceal, he conveys objectively the emotion itself; if there is ever a test on this topic of emotions, he will ace it; if you have to study the science of emotions, live with a child; he will give you the means, the material to reflect and analyze; there is an expression in his eyes when he feels an emotion; it has to be seen so that it can be felt, just like a marvel of nature; he cries at the slightest parting and erupts at the first sign of resurrection; like a gifted musician who plays every measure in its entirety, he plays every emotion, lives it fully, feels it completely. In every act of his we can see how it feels to live an emotion, of how life remains for him and for the thousand others who live, and even if each life has her own unique story to tell, the child speaks of a common theme, a truth that binds us all, like the letters that make up a word, or the words that form a sentence, the poetry behind the prose—in essence the *emotions* themselves.

§

The world of a little child is a world in itself; it must be for how else are we to explain the magnificence, the innocence, the sublimity, the objectivity? The smile of a little child brings wonders to a home, his walk opens the door to every neglected corner in the house; in a small square he can play and find his happiness, and here we see, for a few hundred square feet we sing our anthems to wage a war. What can I say about the child—other than to salute his brilliance? The ways and means he uses to learn and accomplish things is nothing short of a marvel to me. People ask why we cannot win and will over a child of this age, and I say the reason might well be in how he is, in his purity, in his innocence. He wills and wins over us more so than the reverse, just by virtue of being himself, by being true, so that we can see the brilliance of life and the sweetness in it.

§

This language of feelings, even if there is such a thing, must surpass every other language invented—be it of speech, of sign, or even the language found in the symbols of mathematics. This language must be so powerful in itself that perhaps the only way through which we can come close to describe its content must be by the means of perception. Who can narrate to me the power in this content—the feeling itself—not just for a brief time but in continuity? Every poetic verse, every musical composition attempts, but then I meet a child, a child of a tender age of one or two, watch him play, one who has yet to learn a language, yet one who speaks a language that is the best of all—the *language* of perception itself.

§

The first cry of a child as he searches for breath marks the beginning of a journey in the eyes of this world. But life's journey has already begun, in the womb itself, under the care and supervision of nature herself, in her world so to speak, a world far more complex than what we can see, and much more remarkable than what we can imagine. It might well be the reason why when the time comes for the child to leave such a world so he can fill up his lungs with the air from ours, he *begins* his first cry, perhaps his way to signal his parting with nature, and as nature leaves his hand, he grabs another one, the woman herself, to whom he looks up to for all his nursing and care, thus giving her the *will* of what nature has and granting her with what her new birth is—the advent of motherhood.

§

The spirit of the human race is seen majestically in the very young; the unity they portray on their own reflects the commonality found in all, one that we seldom see or hear yet one that we feel deeply; like a work of art they are presented to us in their little body and form, and like an axiom of mathematics they behave; an indulgence in them is an indulgence in a study, of art, of science, of life herself, of living itself—of a genius living in this little life. I can hardly say the same about any man or a woman I have met, but I can confidently assert the genius of a child, not just of a single race, or one culture, but of each and every one, of every land, without even knowing much about the same—the child remains an objective representation in a human form, a pure and clean soul sculpted and carved by the genius of nature.

§

Every genuine smile is a glimpse of happiness; a little child smiles his way to happiness; he has nothing of his own yet he finds the means to be happy; perhaps it is the manner in which he engages with the world—neither taking it seriously nor following it closely. The world charts its own course, but he on the other hand—he *follows* his own imagination, his innate thirst to explore. He labors for his own smile; his eyes and ears work to search and find things, the people he holds dear, and as soon as he finds them, his expression changes, he becomes happy, wears a smile. It feels to me as if this smile is not *entirely* his but simply *derived* from theirs, it lives in his dear ones, hidden beneath their faces all along, which amazingly he first discovers, then extracts, and finally multiplies—first by bringing it on their faces, and then by decking it on his; no matter how they look or what they do he does not care; all he seeks is their presence, their touch. The world may not count his chosen ones as its heroes, but he surely does—such *heartfelt* innocence, such a *praiseworthy* soul. If there is even such a thing called happiness, then it must lie within us or in those we hold dear; it remains our own job to find—just like the child shows; it comes to a form in every episode of closeness, in the company of a dear friend, a pleasant memory, a vivid thought, or even a persuasive study; thoughts must mingle or the hearts must meet for this happiness to come to life—for what is happiness but closeness packed in a smile?

§

The future is unknown, the past fully known. The head is a slave to each, but the heart is to none. The heart beats to a tune, the mood of the present, perhaps doing justice to the fleeting moment that lives in its beat—look at a little child, his head does not bother the heart, for the head knows nothing, and even the heart so little . . . yet the child lives and learns, on his own, by his will, submits to the heartbeat, the whisper in it; why do I need a lesson on living from anyone when the text on living itself narrates right in front of my face, in the child who masters the craft of living, and the art in it—not then but now—neither dwelling on the past nor planning the future, but . . . simply living in the present.

§

A dear possession is cared for deeply, it holds value, but to a little child it means nothing; the moment he lays his eyes on such an object, or for that matter anything new, he grabs and examines—what we admire from a distance, he enjoys up close; to him what good is something sitting in a closet, or engraved on a wall, if it cannot be felt by the power of touch. Give him one and he will show you, he will tear it apart, break it up, or throw it down, and then grab it with his nimble fingers to put it in his little mouth—as if after all he does to that thing, all it needs now is a consolation of a kiss. Like a monarch he *lives*, like an artist he *wills*, no work is dear to him other than the one which he invents on his own. Who is he a slave of? I say no one but himself, his own *imagination*.

§

A daughter is a blessing to a family, to her father she is his world, to her brother she remains a source of lasting comfort, to her mother a mirror of her own self; a daughter brings to a home what nature brings to life—a sweetness, a gentleness, a tenderness; in her early years she is her father's delight, and in his later years she becomes for him his hand of care; the father and his daughter are unique in their own ways, they are opposite in gender, apart in age, and branched in constitution, yet they remain close, like the threads of the same cloth, woven from the same strands, perhaps the reason of this special relationship, one which has evolved into a purest one there is, and one which is man's most divine and clean one—well beyond the powers of my pen to describe. Opposites attract but in this case a father's love and affection towards his own daughter transcends even further, it intensifies with time and offers him a chance to see in her what is never in him—his girl from her bare beginnings—thus giving a meaning to what is theirs, a trust to what is in each—one that he *fiercely* protects, and one that she *fully* grants.

§

A cry is a language in itself; in it lives a feeling, a feeling so deep that it can rarely be expressed in words, the polar opposite of a genuine smile is a heartfelt cry; both of them—the cry and the smile—capture the ends of the swing of human emotions very beautifully; to a child who is just born, the cry remains his lifeline; it's golden, necessary, without it he is crippled, deficient; our ears are tuned to catch this melody, the tone of a cry; we owe a lot to this cry, and while we may belittle it compared to every other act of bravado, in our hearts we always cry even if on our faces we do not—for the heart beats to a melody we first sung, and listens to the language we first spoke—the *persuasive* cry.

§

Every newborn child is a work of art; the arrival highlights nature's methodical creation, it shows her precision, her laborious detail, her meticulousness in what she sets off to do, on her own, away from the eyes and ears of every man; her bold yet simplistic expressions, in those tiny limbs, the clean skin, and a nimble heart, are so powerful in themselves that they can make a man powerless, speechless, spellbound, even the brave pause and admire the arrival of a new life, such is its magnificence and opulence—all done without uttering a single word . . . just how art does.

§

From the first breath to the first step is a majestic show. Every child who accomplishes this milestone does so at his own pace, in his own style; some reach it within a year's time, others take a year more; there is no hurry, no rush, nor any sign of worry seen in a child's demeanor; I reckon even whether the child feels any, all I see is a perpetual willingness—and when his heart shall give the nod he will take his leap of faith. Quite extraordinary, quite remarkable I say, the resolve at such a tender age—he does not compete, neither does he budge. This absence to prove yet this willingness to conquer is a sign of brilliance, an objective mind, a gifted soul in whom lives knowledge in the most pure form; it separates him from the rest by placing him alongside the *truth*—perhaps the reason why every child at this age is an artist in himself; he attempts, he explores, he craves for and carves his own niche, and even if he may reach a milestone a little slower than some of his contemporaries do, he still makes me wonder—what the lack of worry can do to anyone—I dare say it shall elevate them from how they live, to how they are born as—an artist.

§

A child signals a hope; his arrival infuses a new breath in those who hold him dear—he erases their past, forgoes their future; he holds the present so they can enjoy the moment, do justice to his arrival; a disappointment or a triumph pale in comparison to him—it's a marvel of nature embodied in a human form, for me it is nature herself living in plain sight, and even if she cannot converse in a manner I do, she portrays what can be truly felt but can never be fully spoken—the genius within.

§

A one-year-old steps on the grass. She sits down and gets to work—pulling the grass, circling the mud, and even tasting some in her mouth. Such an innate curiosity lives in her, in every little soul of her age, that it's hard to control, to constrain; she has a laser sharp vision, a gifted instinct—I simply stand and watch, I try to control her hands when they go near her mouth, and when I get the slightest inkling of what is to come, I lift her, hold her, and then I hear a cry, loud and clear; she squirms and screams as if I have robbed her of something precious—indeed I must have, I have robbed her of her imagination. Yes, it is the imagination, a wonder of the mind, that helps us aspire, inspire, and even progress; how fortunate it is to see that this imagination lives in abundance in a little child; I take her from the carpet of grass and put her someplace else; the show repeats—imagination always wins, it is not confined to a source, a subject, or a study; the whole world comes together so her imagination can flourish, the world is her text and she its poetry—she brings joy to everyone who holds her dear, but then she also does so much more that I feel she does just to me—she shows me her imagination and in it I find my inspiration.

§

How a newborn life learns to smile is wondrous and magical; it is perhaps nothing short of a miracle; the mechanics of a smile are the same in each, but the expression unique to its own; a simple exercise of the muscle yet a masterpiece when genuine—a completest portrayal of emotions. A tear and a smile remain a child's companions, in absence of a proper language he uses them to convey his needs, his wants; and how well he demonstrates his mastery in each; such completeness, such precision that I feel sometimes this form of speech even surpasses the reach of language; he shows the power of human emotion, the depth it can capture, the range it can conquer. Everyone who cares for him is handsomely rewarded—smile is his nod, tear his nay, and with their interplay he lives his day, sleeps his night, and conveys to them in a manner that no words can—of what they are to him and he is to them.

§

The first year of a child's life is magical; it is perhaps the finest when it comes to learning; there is no one to teach, yet there is ample to learn; and how well does the child live up to the task—the child learns all that he must on his own, by his own; with a tear and a smile he moves along, unwavering, undefeated; he does this in spite of anything and everything; it's as if he is detached from the world, the world exists for him as an object, to tinker, to try, a specimen to study; he dissects and discovers whatever his hands touch. Armed with a eagle's eye, a poet's imagination, an explorer's spirit, and a scientist's curiosity, he lives and breathes; people say there are only a few who can be called a genius, but they fail to see what lives in plain sight: one of nature's prized works, one which she manufactures in plenty, a genius that lives and works in every little child.

§

A piece of magic lives in a little child—in his expression, or in his action. Look at him closely, sit and observe his every act, you will be amazed, perhaps even astonished, by how he learns what he has to learn, by how he lives with what he has got; every experience compels him to express; hunger and pain push him to cry, but satisfy them and you will see life in action; the story of every little child is similar, the life of each one much the same—they live life, fuller and complete I say, forgiving each day, forgetting each night; in the simplest expression of their individuality comes to light the completest portrayal of objectivity. I wonder sometimes what it would be like to retain and replay some of these traits—will our experience enrich us without our comprehension? And then will our minds endeavor, strive, pursue, devote themselves to a study? Perhaps the power of perception will flourish, the artist in us will rejoice; I cannot confirm or deny either but one thing I dare say—we shall live, live our fullest, for what is there to stop us—not even the hesitation of a past disappointment or the laurels of a recent applause; with nothing to haunt, or nothing to pride ourselves on, we shall be, so to speak, in a way fulfilling unfettered nature's will.

§

The curiosity in the early years is one of a kind; it's seen in every life, it repeats in every generation and replenishes itself in the young; it's a constant, a hallmark of our species, the urge to explore, to touch, to see, to walk, and even to think—every century had this and every generation will live it—for so long as nature lives we shall breathe what is hers—the curiosity portrayed beautifully by the very young.

§

The child investigates; she touches and mouths every object her eyes see; this world offers her a stimulation, every object needs her touch, her grab; nothing is dull, everything appears beautiful and remarkable to her senses—nature paints a canvas just for her, and why not, for she is to one of nature's own—energetic, engrossed, exhilarated little soul. I have never seen a child of a year in age being bored, or haunted by boredom; he may cry, vex in the light of the day but I don't believe he is bored at length; distractions help him, cure his fuss—give him a crumpled paper or crumple one and he will smile, the waste in the bin is fun to him; dirt and mud fire his imagination, sand and water color his activity, the dry leaves scattered on the grass delight his eyes, as if their touch soothes his little limbs. He walks on them with majesty, a carpet laid out for a king. Nature employs the simplest of means and the thinnest of methods to keep him busy; a child calms around nature, perhaps even blossoms in it—just like every other life. Isn't this happiness? Or learning—the way it ought to be? A child of a year in age finds his happiness by his own methods; he does not yearn to possess; he borrows only to return, his hands break the things they themselves craft and create, and while he cries at their loss, he wakes the next day with a fresh smile—as if no possession is dear to his heart other than his own act—the act of imagination itself.

§

I enter my home. She watches me and beams with joy; she drops her favorite toy, forgets her cherished activity and leaps towards me; everyone else stays put or greets me with a nod, but she . . . she does something more; she lunges past everyone else to catch my sight, even when she hasn't mastered how to walk; I feel loved, wanted, cared; I turn away to catch my breath, put my things aside, so I can return her favor, but she voices her displeasure—she wants me to hold her now, not a minute from now but now; such is her insistence and persistence. It's a wonderful feeling for a parent when the child behaves in such a manner—for the child sees in clear light the purest relation, one of nature, one given by nature. This is the life of every little child, he finds his world in the world of others, in his parent, his caregiver, or his guardian, and while he may not know a thousand things, he knows one thing and speaks loud and clear—the hands he wishes to hold and the faces he cherishes to see. How objectively a child carries out this relation is astonishing and magical, just think about it, he is objective in his every demand yet in this objectivity he portrays love and affection, warmth and care; there may be hundreds of wonders in this world for my eyes to see, but to me a child of this age tops them all, for he is not just a wonder, but a wonder amongst all wonders—a full living force of nature in flesh and blood.

§

A child of a year in age finds happiness in a jiffy—his curiosity is at its peak and his resolve the strongest. A healthy child makes a happy child, for in so far as he is, and his constitution allows, this age is the age when the world appears beautiful. The fictional characters propel imagination, the pretend play satiates curiosity—in his own world he lives, at his own pace he learns—nothing bothers him, even the world for all its faults and follies fails to dampen his spirit, he lives the simplest yet lives the fullest, a completest portrayal, of a poetry, of a full blooded force—the living genius in the one- year-old child.

§

The milestones of early childhood—cry, smile, roll, sit, crawl, stand, walk, speak—within the first two years of life . . . what is this—nothing but intellectual evolution. Come to think of it, later on everything is simply shaping and molding. If you don't believe in the science of evolution, I suggest you live with a child till he turns two—there is lots to learn and much to see in this time period; difficult to lay it out succinctly; you have to live it—words cannot do justice to any experience, just as every feeling loses some its shine when it is consciously thought.

§

A smile finds a way to a child's face in the easiest of ways; this little soul's world is within the grasp of his eyes, yet his smile has no such boundary; the whole world understands it, reciprocates it; pick him up, play with him, fiddle him around, delight him in your arms and he will reward you with a gift rarely bestowed by our fellowmen—a warm smile, finest there is; even a gloomy day becomes bright, a starry night even starrier, such is the power—he gives what every life needs, and speaks with ease what can never be spoken—a genuine smile.

§

A little child waves at a figurine, a statuette; I see many young children, around a year of age, barely walking, mostly babbling, pass by my alley smiling and waving at the decorations I have laid out on the grass; some get lost in the color and the shape, others enthralled by their action and the movement; it's a wonderful show for them, entertaining and magical I think; sure it's Christmas, but these young minds—do they know such a thing called Christmas? I say no; they do not and frankly they don't even care: It's not the festival that brings a smile on their face, but something more, something else; far richer, far more powerful than the God we search; we look for a God in every festival we celebrate, in every hymn we pray, a God we have yet to find, but they, they do so much more; they see in every festival what lives in plain sight, what needs to seen, the highest form—the art itself.

§

A work of art conveys a gist, reflects a truth; every life in its early years reveals a lot; longing, belonging, happiness, joy, tears, smiles—are seen in bounty in those nimble years, even on the smallest separation the child cries his heart out, the smile on his face after taking his first step is a feeling of accomplishment—what is all this but the portrayal of emotions, of life nevertheless; the myriad, colorful forms depicted day after day innocently, vigorously in this small span of early childhood—this is poetry, a work of art, for observe any child of around a year, listen to him, see him, linger with him, study him and you will see life speaking to you in its fullest—about how she is and all that she has.

§

The young infant is nothing short of a marvel, this specimen so to speak is manufactured in thousands a day, yet every arrival of his speaks of a certain triumph, a triumph of nature—man intervenes when he must and where he should but it is nature who runs this show, in her care, under her watch, a tiny cell grows into a full human, the transcendence from the inanimate to an animate, a microscopic to a macroscopic; this is an evidence in plain sight of the rules of nature, the derivation of life, from a single kernel, the same source—in nature lives life and conversely in every life a part of nature.

§

A newborn child who has just learnt to smile is one of awe; pure delight I say to watch; smiling is a quintessential expression of something pleasant, something warm, an enjoyment of a moment, or perhaps even a hope of what it is to come, or a memory of the past; yet for all these reasons we smile, to a child a smile is simple and pure; in that smile lives a tender human being, a longing, an acceptance, a submission of thankfulness to those hands—hands who have cared, hands who have toiled for a life other than theirs. A father comes home from a hard day of labor, and his year-old son greets him with a smile; this smile is a magnet of sweetness, an embrace to our self, a meeting of loved one lost long time ago; the joy in this greeting is one of kind—earthly yet heavenly—how can the child go on to do this with such ease what a man who has lived so long rarely does—a genuine smile—no wonder in all our mingling and conversations we can make out a genuine smile from a counterfeit—for we did it once and hence we can do it now. I say, let's do it now.

§

There came a chance when my son was born, a chance I got from nature, a hope which still lives in me; years have gone by but it feels like yesterday, when his hands lay on mine, his head touched mine; I was his world then, but who am I to kid—he now slips away from a boy to become what I am—a man. The time has changed, the age has passed, yet the place remains the same; he searches for his friends in the light of the day, he wanders in his thoughts more than he wonders on mine, his play is dearer to his heart than my silly game, and while I wait patiently on my couch so he can come and ask, I realize I have to wait, be waiting, till the day draws to a close. For no fault of his he is now his own, the world pulls him more than I can ever so; even the jest that once made him laugh now fails to tap his busy ears, just the same way I was perhaps then, so like a rule this follows on to me, a necessity I say, the necessity of life. For a father this is his destiny, his plight to bear, his child will hold his hand only to leave, yet in this parting I see a resurrection, an immense satisfaction, a plenitude of memories, one that I thank him for, one that nature entrusted me with, and one that I shall faithfully serve till my very end—my fatherhood.

§

What a world a young child portrays by himself—a world of objectivity, of innocence, of art, of resilience, of tenderness; in his presence he brings in people a unity, a oneness, one of a kind and one of a class. Like a speech that bonds everyone, or a musical score that speaks to each, or a work that unites minds of every generation . . . he does this all, by the thinnest of means and the simplest of methods, employing a simple arithmetic and proceeding to solve the equation of living—by living himself; the multiple emotions of life are illustrated in a single show. Is this a glimpse of greatness, of a class, the inner workings of nature herself? Perhaps so, for in every action of his, is a spectacle—his tears end and follow up with his smile, minute after minute varied emotions come to play like the colors of a rainbow, or the seasons of nature; he falls one minute, rises the next, living every hour as if new; he wakes up crying yet with the slightest touch of hands he smiles with warmth; neither knowing anyone's name nor their trade, just knowing who are his, he lives his day and sleeps his night—this is his world, a world so pure and clean that I say it is the finest there is, a world that this world ought to preserve and protect—the world of every child.

§

A child of a few months finds a familiar voice in the melody of music; looking at him it becomes clear he can feel the pulse of music, like the pulse of life, this distinction between music and the rest comes naturally to him, innately to his senses; to me this is his first lesson on speech, which when broken down is a musical wave, of sharps, of tones, of harmonics, perhaps the reason for this wonderful expression in every act he does—his cry, or his smile—for he lives and breathes the language of the heavens—music.

§

The art of learning music comes naturally to young children, more easily than it takes for a grown man to master. The further from childhood we begin to learn the first lesson in music, the harder is the climb, requiring days to perfect what a willing boy or girl can accomplish in a few hours. While a man can show his prowess in every other trade or vocation, when it comes to music, it is the child who wins our heart with his poise and performance. It is not so much of what the child performs, but the ease with which he learns this fine art, from how little he knows about the world and its workings, suggesting that music lives in a world of its own, a divine cottage or a heavenly home where it dwells in peace and permanence. The remoteness of music and its absolute alienation from all of man's affairs and his aims helps in it being *pure* and *clean*, and how befitting it is that childhood is granted the swiftness to learn and master this wonderful art faster than any phase of our life, as childhood as it so happens, stays away from all of man's vanity and his wickedness, thus being *pure* and *clean*.

§

She looks at me, the little one who is nearing a year, she smiles to everyone she knows, jumping herself to her brother without a fear, her mother for a laugh; she teases and tinkers on every new object that her eyes see, and then as I sit beside her restless soul, she converses in her babbles about her story, which I think is her study—alas I have no clue of the depth of her thoughts, or what she is trying to convey; it may be a chatter or something profound, her eyes fixated on the object itself, trying to grab, touch, and see—is she a scientist, an artist, a philosopher? I say she is a little of each, a learner first and foremost, the finest one there is, one which my mortal mind cannot grasp and one which this busy world ought to see.

§

A child of a year accomplishes a lot, he perfects and practices on his own, by himself, without the world watching; sometimes it may happen his first roll is not his first, his first clap may his second, his stand his fourth; the first of the firsts he may have done it on his own, celebrated a certain victory on his own, jubilated on his own, without the world watching; it is almost an exemplary demonstration on the habit of work, how working ought to be—forget the world, let us work because we will, only for our will—no less, no more.

§

There is a smile on the face of a child when he senses familiarity; in the first few months it is the touch and then slowly graduates to a face, a person—the perceptual makes way to the intellectual, the touch to the thought.

§

The first step for a child calls for a celebration; true this fact but let's go back in time when the child learnt to stand . . . what did he do? He tapped his feet as if giving a signal, a vote of thanks, a cue to his very own, a mother who holds his feet, a mother who grants every life a chance to walk her treasured lands between her vast seas, a mother whose soil breathes a source of life and whose dust the remains of it, a mother to us all—this Mother Earth.

§

The child learns to crawl; he gets adept at this craft, crawls to every nook and corner of the house; active and alert, his eyes watch for the slightest movement, his ears tune to a pin drop; and once he sets off, a primitive urge takes over, he mouths what he will soon touch; observe him from a distance you will see a lion in him, in his gait or his gaze and why not? A lion hearted spirit lives in his tiny soul.

§

The sight of a little child who has just learnt to stand is one of a kind; there is a smile on the child's face when he accomplishes such a feat, he is inwardly happy and outwardly joyous expressing it in the most wonderful of emotions, pure delight I say, which can bring a smile to any face; with a clap of his hands or a tap on his feet he conveys his firsts; and even if he falls the next moment, he will stand, he shall rise, for his feet are held by his very own—this Mother Earth.

§

A child of a year babbles in the simplest of voices; there are no words to express his speech, yet his speech stands out as one; he conveys, condenses every feeling in a unique babble, a sound similar in modulation found in every creation of nature—isn't he just as simple as them yet having a magnificence of each; it must be true for whenever he encounters them—*her creations*—he gets lost in their company; it's as if he has found what he has been looking for—the spirit of nature.

§

The early years of life are a joy to watch, in a jiffy we can make a little one smile, make him forget; this immediate transition is remarkable and nourishing for any soul—on how it elevates him from all the rest; such a little soul yet such a big heart who can wean off a teary cry and wear it into a beautiful smile.

§

Why does my heart rejoice when it sees a simple show—the taps with her feet, the babbles from her lips, or the touch of her hands? It's as if my heart is fortunate to witness this episode, hence it leaps and expresses itself, thankful for a clean and a majestic show of life; every emotion is objectively portrayed, a pain with a cry, happiness with a smile, no concealment, no counterfeit; the heart knows this, it has known it all along, and when it sees such a show it speaks—not by any impression with the words, but by the expression in the eyes.

§

A child around the age of one is an adventurer; he explores, touches, grabs everything that lies in his way; and then when he perfects the art of standing we see a glimpse of his energy, his optimism. A new life springs in him, the world awaits his touch, every attraction urges him, and as he finds the courage to take his first step he lends this world a hope—what a kindred spirit this little soul is, neither does he know much about this world nor does he know how it works, yet he finds the willingness to learn, to see, to enjoy every object that meets his eye.

§

A newborn child cries; hunger or pain is conveyed through a cry; a cry of persuasion, a cry of a plea, a cry as impassioned as it can be, as desperate as it can get, so much so that every ear listens, every eye looks—the cry is all he knows, all he has got, and all he will use till he learns to speak, till he reasons so to speak, this bare language allows him to survive, and even thrive; we may not think much about a cry, but it is the cry which every parent wishes to hear moments after their child is born, for in this cry is his first breath, a gesture of life, nature's speech and a signal of an arrival of a pure soul on this treasured Earth.

§

An old neighbor sits on the porch; a baby is born down the street; the baby grows as the old man ages; one sprinting with the freshness of life, the other nearing his end; they meet on one of his slow walks; the baby waves as the old man smiles—do they know each other? Absolutely not. Is she one of his? Certainly no. Yet he lets out his hand to grab hers, hold her little fingers, thus unknowingly highlighting a fact—every little life has in it a fresh breath, an objective stance, an instinctive urge and an intellectual potential, in essence a bright hope, which the withering old see in the new.

§

A child to me is an illustration of a rule, a rule of life, a necessity of nature. In those early years there is a wealth of material to be seen in his every action, his crawl, his babble, his gaze, or his step; the way he commissions his every need as a want is phenomenal; he begins his life bare and naked yet he wins the heart, nothing to show, nothing to speak, yet his actions convey in the completest form an innocence—a innocence that melts our heart so much that our arms reach out to his for an embrace ... who is he? I say a living genius.

§

A child who has learnt to crawl and started to grab is an explorer in himself; a daredevil we may say who knows nothing of danger as he can't think of one; a fall, a hurt, or a cry does not dampen his spirit; nothing comes in his way; he stands up crippled nevertheless, yet undefeated and unwavering showing the world what he is made of, an unmatched resilience, and the world obliges, clapping and cheering his every move. He has nothing of his own other than his own self, yet he wills. Where does he find this will, this willingness? It must be from a world far superior than ours or else it would not be so novel in every occurrence; he is like a comet that lights up the sky, a beacon of hope in the mediocrity that so abounds—people go at lengths to see something spectacular, they travel through valleys, climb hills, conquer mountains so a marvel of nature meets their eye, but then for me—there she stands on her two little feet in front of my eyes showing me in the clearest of light of how nature is, her spirit, her resilience, her endurance, her art, her beauty, her grace all condensed in her tiny little soul.

§

There are seven wonders of this world and seven seas to cross; a lot is talked about them, books written, pictures taken, speeches given, and while they are indeed landmarks to see, what remains to me a finest piece of nature's work is a newborn child. It is not just his growth that happens under her care that stumps me to the fullest, but the way he learns that makes it all the more astonishing—right from his first breath to his first step. It's a wonder for me, a manufacture of nature, available in plenty for our eyes to see, living among each one of us, showing what a genius nature is—a stamp of superiority, of authoritativeness, ingrained in his little soul.

§

A child's company brings out the child in us; we have a mind of our own yet we follow his tune; seldom is this seen with our fellowmen to whom we must look rational and reasonable but to a child we need not worry; wealth and fame do not mean much to him, our conquests have no currency, they are pale to his demands; all he looks for is a hand to hold, lips to sing, legs to dance; he sees us just the way he sees everyone, a life in itself, a life of action, of movement—one he can play with and one he can learn from.

§

The first of firsts in a child's life marks a rapid progression—the first cry, the first roll, the first crawl, or the first step—it's an action on the part of a child, where it signals a progress—one that begins under nature's care and ends in her watch. As she leaves his hand, she leaves a hope, a hope seen in every child's face, a hope she wishes the world will make good of by giving her life a chance, a chance so that her little life will prevail to walk the vast lands of this treasured Earth.

§

Leisure lives in a child—perhaps the reason for his astonishing accomplishments in a short span. In those early years before the child turns two, a child's method of learning is nothing short of amazement, inspiration, and consolation—amazement because he does it on his own, inspiration because he wills without a care or a worry of this world, and consolation because it happens by the hand of nature who instills in him what she abundantly has—her kindred spirit.

§

Trust—a promise—comes naturally to a newborn child. The child trusts his caregiver, his guardian, his parent without the slightest hesitation, not just in episodes but in totality, placing his bare life in their hands; we may say the child has no choice or a say in the matter but still this act of his highlights a teaching, a teaching he has learnt well before he takes his first breath, a teaching ingrained and imbibed in every life as it cares for the young and the new, a teaching of the dependence of a life in the hands of the other. Trust—a word—when taken to the heart works like magic, hands join, things move, work gets done, as the reliance is on something far more valuable, on one's word, a handshake more than any bond on paper; our hearts rejoice when we see this in action, we pause and admire when such a story finds its way to our ears, or even in theatre when trust is portrayed in its finest form, there is elation and embrace when we witness such an act, and likewise anger and disgust when treachery gets the better of trust. Through these acts we can see how similar we are; it must be for we have known it ever since we were small and little—the essence of the word trust—of what it is, a hope of nature herself, which each one of us *is*, and her innate quality, which each one of us *has*.

§

There is fearlessness and ferocity in a child who has learnt to crawl; every new object needs to be seen, touched, grabbed, and mouthed—it's an amazing show, and although tiresome to the caregiver a brilliant exhibition to anyone and everyone who watches it closely; this raw optimism, innate urge, and ingrained necessity is a spark of genius—which somehow shows up in full force and luster well before the child begins to speak to or learn from any man.

§

A young one who has learnt to crawl keeps the home busy; the need to see, touch, grab comes to him instinctively; and whether he does it in the confines of his home, or in the safety of his garden, for him it is an exploration of a whole new world. With every such undertaking the need grows, it intensifies with time, culminates and finds a home in each one of us, the need to explore, to travel—in essence our own wanderlust.

§

The first step of a child is among the firsts of life; it's a small step for the child but a proud moment for the father; in those humble beginnings lie high hopes; for it means the child commences his journey of what will be his own; the hope that he will walk the vast lands and sail the high seas of this treasured Earth.

§

The magnificence of nature comes to life with a full force in the early years of childhood; child and nature go hand-in-hand during this period; curiosity abounds, learning soars, action abets, tenacity wills, and tenderness lasts during this time; amazingly every accomplishment happens without much intervention by any man; a man can do only so much, as the child cries, smiles, turns, sits, crawls, stands, walks, runs, speaks, in essence learn on his own without a book or a bible. It is nature's brilliance, a brilliance handed down to the child by nature herself, a brilliance found in every little heart, his one and only one teacher—his only God—to whom he diligently *listens* and from whom he willingly *learns*.

§

Curiosity abounds in childhood. In the earlier years, children are curious about the world itself; they sense, smell, touch, grab, mouth everything the eyes see; how easy it is to bring a smile to a child's face—show them something new and there they go—smile adorns their cheeks, happiness decks the face. Even a cry, a hurt, or a nagging pain vanishes when curiosity takes over. Shall we say then that every soul who retains this curiosity has found the means to remain happy, for only when our curiosity ends do we look at the world from a different lens, whereas the child looks at the world like an artist does—for what it is; in essence for his enjoyment rather than for his profit.

§

A child in the first year, perhaps the second, wins and wills over everyone; he does what he wishes, lives like he wants; other than care and nourishment he asks none, there is nothing more any of us can give, or for that matter teach; on the other hand, he teaches us, recites to us the text on living, portrays for us life itself, laying out in the clearest of light of all what a life comprises, the emotions in it, the expressions of it; like a gifted artist who projects every color in a painting, or a versatile composer whose music enumerates every emotion, just that this little soul does all of it without any aid—by the mere act of living itself.

§

The instinct to live is vigorously manifested in the first few years of every life; a child learns on his own everything he must, precisely, perfectly, persistently—a mastery of a method, one from the book of nature. Yet in spite of this willingness, the ferocity, the will to survive, there lives in him a beautiful innocence, thus highlighting to us an innate character of life. How come much later the situation is different, the instinct to live and learn with the same zeal and curiosity is taken for granted, a laxity that perhaps costs us our innocence? Alas we are in the company of men now, those who will judge us and those who we must judge. The world catches up on its mischief and for all its reasons robs us of this innocence—one that nature lends, and one that a child lives and breathes with in the early years of childhood.

§

Around the age of six or seven months in a child's life, there is a marked transition; every new face a child sees has a reticent effect on the child's mood; this behavior is rampant in some children more so than others. An incoming stranger, an infrequent visitor, or for that matter a more frequent guest is treated cautiously by the child, an attempt to receive a handsome smile is a hard task, an uphill climb, a vain undertaking; the child in arms does not oblige, he looks cautiously, harboring a curious tone, voicing his displeasure at the slightest touch; his hands cling to his parent, his eyes reveal a discomfort, and his little head turns away to rest on the shoulders as if saying to the stranger—"Whoever you are, you still have to earn my trust. You may be famous, you may be brave, you may be rich, an emperor or a prince, a scholar, or for that matter a priest, a prophet, perhaps God even," the child continues, "yet in all your glory my world is not in yours, it belongs to these who have cared for me, looked after me, and listened to me." Why this happens, how this happens is remarkable and consoling; consoling for the parent as the child has made it clear to this world where his world truly lies, whose hand he wishes to hold, who have become his and who haven't, and remarkable because all this happens without any learning or teaching from anyone—time and nature impart this knowledge to the child—the kin he belongs and the bond he forms with those souls who have toiled and cared for him day after day, night after night.

If this is not an expression of loyalty, thankfulness, and gratitude then what is?

§

How come the babbles of a child attract all ears, enthrall every audience? It's as if the tone has a magical composition, a precise measure of length and harmony, so much so that it aligns everyone around; we get along, fold our legs, sit next to the child and become one of his; in such a tone is perhaps the mystery of language, the idea of a thought, for it is universal, objective, and might I add even heavenly. For a parent it is a wonder of delight, and to a thinker a material of ideas, a window into a world of genius—the child himself.

§

A newborn child is a child of nature first before he is one of ours; it's in her world that he takes a form, becomes a shape, and grows in size; even his first breath or his first cry is an illustration of her teaching; he masters the art, perfects the technique, in her care, under her watch, holding her hand—over here among us, in this world so to speak, he learns to reason; what is necessary has already been imparted and imbibed by her—the will, the willingness; no wonder this world can never impart such a teaching; it can help us discover, but then it must stop, for then her lessons take over, the willingness comes to life, the will begins to speak, our reason finds a medium to express, thus showing each of us what each of us can be; in effect we exhibit a purpose—an expression of what we live for and one that we die with.

§

The innocence of a child in the first few years is one to behold, the curiosity in it one to learn, and the willingness is one to follow—it is perhaps nature herself incarnated in a soul, speaking through this form about the universality of life—the falls, the cries, the smiles, the tears have an unusual power in them; they win our hearts and rule our heads; for who else can in a single stroke yield such a distinct message, the essence of which we fully grasp without the need of any book or a bible, it's how life is and how she remains at her core; this is genuine display, a poetic narration, a brilliance of a superhuman class through the eyes of the little child—the genius of nature.

§

The initial years, the first, and even the most part of the second, are somewhat magical in a human life; they highlight vividly a spark of nature, a fierce expression in everything a life does; this phase is poetry in motion, an elegant and a masterful performance from a life who knows nothing about this world yet lives as if it is well versed on the text of living. How can we teach such a soul anything? All we can do is look after its every need and watch its show; yes he cries, he swivels, the moods vary, but then he is genuine, more than any man or woman, a hope for this world, a divine form who lives among us, who rejoices in our arms, delights the heart with his play; people go at length in search of God but then there it stands—a marvel and a wonder of art—carved and sculpted by one and only one—nature herself.

§

The cry of a child is sensitive to the ear, the tones express a mood, the modulation conveys a want, it remains a child's only language, a simple yet a powerful one in itself, one that ensures his survival, and one that even surpasses the fluency of speech, a direct and a terse manifestation of the emotion therein; a child learns to smile much later, first he must cry as he makes the passage, perfect the art of crying in the months that follow; and for this reason we can confidently assert why a tear will always move us more than any smile, why comedy can never fill the gulf that tragedy had left, for a cry is given whereas a smile acquired, a cry is ordained, a decree, a will, handed down to every life by nature herself—the sole witness of everything this world has and anything a life shows—animate or inanimate.

§

The first few years of infancy are all about the little child; the moods, the movements and the mannerisms are one of a kind, perhaps the finest, they stand out in-spite of everything this world has or anything the world shows. In those early years the child in itself bears a striking resemblance to every other work of nature, a perfection to admire, a company to behold; the child's gaze catches our eyes, the coos bring a music to our ears, the touch boons a heavenly feel; every accomplishment becomes an occasion to celebrate, likewise every fall is easily begone; the world suddenly appears beautiful, people likable, strangers pause and adore this young creation, smile and wave in cheer and glee; everyone comes together to enjoy, to be enjoyed; hands join, eyes meet, ears listen; in effect a house becomes a home; movement and action reign and rule; happiness finds a place to rest, and joy fills our hearts—this little wonder shows all of us what we always look for but fail to see—the genius of life.

§

Life is straightforward for a newborn child; no airs, no pride, everything he does is done because he must, an act of pure learning; every fall, every cry, even every accomplishment is forgotten without much ado, or a fuss; each day is a new birth, a fresh start, a humble beginning, just like the rising sun, and perhaps it is this genuine effort, the necessity to never give up that gives the child his glow—for behind that tender face lies a firm resolve, a lionhearted spirit, an iron will, and a steady hand, the hand of nature herself, as she guides his each step, his every endeavor; it's their show, one of her *will* and the other of his *willingness* that not only wins our heart but also awakens in us what our fellowmen seldom do—our individual therein.

§

In the early years of infancy a child is a subject of learning; neither can anyone teach the child what he has to learn nor can anyone discipline the method of learning itself; the child learns all that he must simply on his own—smiling, rolling, crawling, sitting, standing, walking, talking, and so on; learning swiftly, handsomely, and willingly; here we see the reason why, the difference in teaching therein, in the means and method employed, in the teacher itself, who is none other than nature herself; nature holds the child's hand tight and firm, and while she is in charge who are we to stand between the two—a master of a heavenly class and a pupil in an obedient form—so they can put on a show to behold—an exemplary illustration of brilliance, of a genius. Might we write a rule: Only a genius, nature herself, can teach another one of its kind, the child himself.

§

There is seen a perceptive glance in every newborn child once the child gets acquainted with the world and accustomed to all that it has to show. Everything the eyes see is new; every creation of nature or for that matter even of a man holds the gaze; the child gets lost in the art and the aesthetics therein, fixed on the object thereof; to some this glance may appear as a casual look or a fleeting play of the eyes, but on a close observation it reveals much more than that, it bears the stamp of contemplation, of perception, of a certain reflectiveness where it feels like the child searches for what the thing is, or how the phenomenon represents; in effect the child is philosophizing for a brief time as necessitated by his age, that is to say thinking, like an artist, or a poet who lingers, stretches his imagination beyond the seen or the heard, yet being direct and clear—a hallmark of real and proper philosophy. How astonishing and liberating it is to see that such a little life who has not even lived to a year is equipped to think, to learn, simply by observation and imitation; to me the child is a lone artist who works in *seclusion* yet learns by *inclusion*, alternating between the two from time to time, as and when needed; *with* a single glance the child speaks a ton about the ability of the human mind, the reach of human thought, and *through* that glance the child looks for a chance, a chance so he can flourish as he enters into what has been hailed as a poetic period, a time of vivid imagination, of objective contemplation—the years of childhood—a chance that this world *promises* and hence one that this world *owes*.

§

A newborn child has nothing of his own to speak of or to show from, yet he holds the attention of anyone and everyone who pass by and notice him; we may say he is fragile needing the care, the comfort, the warmth of our arms; and while this is indeed true what he ends up doing for each and every one of us is much much more than what he asks; every playful encounter with him is an indulgence with something heavenly; he plucks out from our head the endless wants solely with his gaze, and as if this was not enough he then proceeds to stop the world for us simply by his smile, *so we can see life in her most pure form*, of how she *is*, what she *has*, her raw and nimble expression before this world stakes its claim, thus leaving us inspired and even enriched, something only a genius can do, evident in every tiny human soul.

§

An abuse to a child's life, what shall we call this act – humanity's darkest and demonic expression that there is. If this life is a blessing, then how come its creator—nature—allowed such a thing to happen, for isn't she the almighty, the all powerful force behind everything that there is . . . but what if she is not . . . she has to do what she must . . . then whom can we put the blame on—the man himself or a much superior force—a God perhaps; such a man is punished for his sins and lives his life in humiliation and misery, but this does not help the case, the saga continues, history repeats, every generation who walks this Earth witnesses such barbaric and cruel acts—How come? Why so? We can lament on Man's behavior or resign to God's helplessness, but we always marvel on a Child's persona; such is its preeminence and power. So then shall we say that the child must be God like? To those who say God lives in children I must say it is perhaps the other way around, for if we place this almighty God on a sacred pedestal, then we will diminish the meaning of what is sacred, thus diminishing the life we can always see—the sacred life of the little child. Man spills blood for the very God he may never see, forgetting what makes his God a God, the child, if there is any hope of a God . . . then a child must live in such a God.

§

A newborn child follows art and engages in music; a colorful object captivates the eye, a soothing melody engages the ear; his gaze is fixed on a work of art as if he searches for the meaning therein, while his eyes invariably calm in comfort when a soothing melody falls on his ears; this fresh life illustrates in the clearest of light the importance of art and music, the richness they bring in, the universality they speak of, essentially highlighting for us a world where they truly belong—a world of permanence. Even mathematics for all its might bows down to these illustrious fields—for mathematics strives to prove what art invariably reflects and music essentially speaks—the composition of the world itself.

§

The babbles of a young child convey a text, a text of animation, of an eagerness, a propensity to show, and a willingness to learn; we marvel and enjoy looking at this delightful phase of infancy, a poetic period, when all the needs are taken care of, or all the wants fulfilled, and how well does the child use this to his good—he learns what nature wishes, masters what she wants—an exemplary pupil who gives each of us what each of us needs—a beautiful hope.

§

In every new life is a seen a spark, a necessity, an objective semblance to the potential of life. Hence those early years are a marvel and delight to every parent or caregiver; in those golden years learning happens naturally and willingly, perception influences action, care is reciprocated by a genuine smile, every possession is let go as soon as it vanishes from the sphere of the eye; it is only when the child understands his identity, essentially when the I starts to talk, that we can see the influence of reason; in essence we can say that this identity gives the child his ego and marks the beginning of the reversal from the objective to the subjective—the gradual growth of the ego—which ripens as childhood departs and finally roars to announce what is the age of manhood.

§

Every newborn child speaks a language that each of us fully grasps, and likewise each of us can indulge in a play just like he is our own; the child shows how similar each one of us is, no matter how different we may look, or how divergent our language, nationality, or even our culture remains; this wonder of wonders is a symbol of objectivity just like every other work of nature is; every great work of art, of music, or even of knowledge, hints and reflects what this freshly minted life exemplifies by living itself—the universality of our race, the commonality of life, reciting in the most primitive and raw form—nature's text—loud and clear.

§

The bond between a mother and her child in the initial months highlights a teaching largely unappreciated; a lesson that gets manifested vigorously in the early months of a child's life—one that can never be imparted by any human soul. The manner in which a newborn child finds his way to his mother's chest is a wonder in itself—for it demands a certain knowledge the child must already have, one that he must have learnt from someplace else—in the lap of nature herself—well before he takes his place in this world we call our own. He looks at his mother with hopeful eyes, making an impassioned plea, a persuasive cry, wanting the only thing from all the things this world has, her breast—which he knows is the source of all his nutrition as well as his nourishment. The mother obliges to his will, giving in to his demand, his every craving, and as his lips latch on her chest so he can quench his thirst, he also finds what he has been looking for—safety and comfort—perhaps reminiscing about a time from the womb—the breast now being the cord. This scene is an expression of the delicate nature of life, yet it happens to be the most resilient, for it shows how the two of them—the mother and her child—live through their struggles day after day, night after night, immersed in each other, meshed as one; she puts her heart in his care, he in return places his life in her hands; she lives for him, while he from her, and for everything she does so that he can become his own, he repays her back with all and the only wealth he has—his *first* smile.

§

A social interaction is almost absent in the early months of a child's life; it is restricted to a chosen few, yet the child learns all that he must by the act of observation and imitation; he perfects all the tasks at hand by his own will, without any care or worry about the world, what the world might think, or what it shall say; a child engrossed is a child immersed in his own study, a picture of concentration, indulged in everything the world shows yet somehow detached from it, purposefully, deliberately as if to keep a certain sanctity and purity about himself. This little life shows each and every one of us the power of individuality, the strength of our inborn will, which is lent by nature herself—what one can do if necessity preceded it—the effort behind and the leap forward—a lesson for every adventure, in every pursuit—one we can use in every walk of life—for in the end what is life other than a valiant attempt?

§

Looking at a newborn child we can see what a marvel nature has manufactured, and how pale and mundane the affairs of this world are in comparison to her magnificent piece of work—this very young life. This work of art lives true to its word just like every other work of nature does—inspiring, elevating, comforting even consoling; in effect what we see in a child is a recital of a text on living itself, spoken by nature herself, through the eyes of that young child, so much so that not even grief can stop the child from doing what it must—which is learn—showing us how learning ought to be—void of vanity, free from wickedness—a hallmark of infancy and the years of early childhood.

§

Music—an art difficult to master yet easy to follow—is swiftly learnt—insofar as the ability goes—in the years of childhood; it's as if this fine art, the skill and dexterity it demands, can be perfected in those tender years, a hint and a wonderful analogy to what childhood strives to be—divine and heavenly.

§

A new life sleeps and nurses most of the time, yet when awake and playful he dazzles and delights everyone around him. In that hour of play he ensures anyone and everyone who indulges with him is rewarded handsomely; his coos, his babbles delight the eyes and soothe the ears; such is the power of his speech, perhaps so because he recites for us a page from nature's vast text, unabridged, unedited, animated, organic, and lively; they say that the secrets of this world are in the skies—and we need to study the heavens to uncover them—but I say they reside right here, in front of our eyes, in every new life, available to us for study, through which nature speaks of how she *is* and the essence of all that she *has*.

§

The sighting of a familiar face brings joy to a newborn; it is our good fortune that children—the very young at least—can bring on our faces in a jiffy what lies deep in our hearts—a honest expression, a rare smile; one whose power can strengthen bonds, kindle friendships, break barriers, and even win hearts. The question remains: If ever nature has to find a home where she can dwell fair and free, who would she choose and where would she go?—I reckon it must be in the child—for the child acts and enacts just as she wishes and lives and breathes just like she wants.

§

A woman has been endowed with a quality that is distinctly her own; it is handed down to a woman by none other than nature herself; a woman brings to form the ideas that nature has, growing from a tiny cell a whole new life, yet under nature's watchful eyes; and with the coming of a new life, which then a woman nurtures and nourishes, nature speaks through that woman's child about a world, a world that is nature's own, a world superior in every aspect to the one we live in, a world of infinite and eternal ideas, a world that even if not free from strife and suffering remains pure and sublime, and a world that every newborn child retains and reflects as he lives in ours, for each and every one of us to watch in awe and linger in delight.

§

A newborn life is a lasting expression of individuality; of how he lives and breathes needing only a few hands to care; with neither any friend nor any foe he sets off learning on his own all what he must—his instinct being his master and his senses his companion; it is perhaps the gravest of errors to neglect and overlook the work a new life achieves in early years of childhood, the genius therein, how a newborn child accomplishes in a few years the methods necessary for him to live, and why not, for in a child nature lives with her vigor and vibrancy, she speaks showing her ideas—the unparalleled spirit, the childlike pursuit, the essence of everything sincere and genuine, and perhaps the essence of her text on how she wishes each of us must live.

§

A child represents nature's objective text; in it we can as far as we can see the representation of nature's own work, a clean picture untainted by the hands of this world; the genius of this child unwraps day by day, as he lives every moment as it should be lived; for pain he cries, for pleasure he smiles, and through them our eyes watch and ears listen; he smiles as if everything is anew, forgetting every cry with ease. The jewel of our intelligence—reason—is underdeveloped or even absent in a new life; yet every new life that comes into our own is a genius in itself, demonstrating that reason alone is not enough, for all its might reason falls short to win our hearts—like a poet who pens eternal lines without ever learning the rules of poetry.

§

A newborn comes into this world with nothing but his breath, he comes bare and naked, yet he has something in *himself*—a divine purity—which no one in this world can lay their hands on, it remains his and is well beyond the reach of a tribe or a nation, a culture or a race; no amount of wealth from this world can buy it, nor any level of fame can grant it its due; it is so to speak the expression of a place he comes from, perhaps the kernel of nature herself—a place from where every life *begins* and a place to where every life *ends*.

§

A newborn speaks in the same tone in every culture, and a mother nurtures her own child in the same manner in every land; this is one of humanity's most innocent and genuine expressions—children play with each other in spite of their race or color and a woman nurtures all her children in the same way irrespective of her own race or color.

§

The cry of a newborn child is desperate yet relieving; every ear yields to one, it unknowingly takes us back to our origins, for why else do we fully grasp such a tone in full and final? It is the expression of a place, a place from where everything begins and the one where everything ends.

§

This world with its countless aims and cycles passes by our eyes; life comes and goes, people strive and suffer, yet every child who makes his way into this world and lends it his breath blesses it as if ordained; he is so to speak a marvel beyond anything this world has, as he brings into this world a hope, a new beginning, and a chance for the world to see once again life and her great show—of her vigor, her vitality, and her versatility.

§

A newborn speaks only one language, of a cry, which if we are to deliberate is a musical sequence in itself, a music so fine and persuasive, distinct and clear, that it never needs a lesson, a teaching, or a sermon; this tune comes to us because music lives within us in its entirety; yet in spite of it being so personal, music remains universal; it appeals to everyone, aspires to each, doing what many a men cannot do; it unites us, binds us, showing us how similar we are, and how rightly so, for in our bare beginnings, our first breath, we all spoke in the same vein the same verse—the *cry* of music.

§

A child is closer to nature than a man is, for the child comes from a place which a man has fully forgotten; quite the reason why early childhood seldom finds the need to be with nature, for nature lives in a child in all her spirit and vigor, preparing him to face the daunt that is yet to come, and perhaps giving herself a hope that when the child grows into a man, he can repay the favor by living with a spirit that she embodies, one that she left in him in the heydays of his childhood.

§

Life has a peculiar way of showing us how she has to be really lived, only after we have progressively lived through our current age does she highlight the value of the previous; nothing is known beforehand, she insists we live out our weals, our woes so we can earn the wisdom therein; yet in all the rabble and noise that goes on with the business of living, life sometimes paints for us a picture of childhood, which we may have seen or felt, the poetic age when energy, vitality, and vigor are at their peak, where the will thrives without much ado, and what the world does holds little meaning, above all a lionhearted spirit—the secret of how she wishes she has to be really lived.

§

The child knows so little but he lives as if he is well versed in the text of living; he lives and breathes without a care or a worry, his heart rejoices in the play of dirt and mud, his head does not reason yet he is full of glee, *he finds joy where a man cannot*, and why not, for he behaves just as nature asks, and for this willingness he shows, nature lets him in on her secret and lends him her vigor—the freshness of which is seen on his face.

§

The simplicity of life paradoxically makes its comprehension difficult. We are born from the same cradle of nature yet we end up living uniquely by our ways. Minimize every moment to a rule, an equation and sum it overall, all of life, species, I say we have cleanest objectivity. The rules are the same, derived from the same kernel, the same source of truth—they have to be, look at a new life, the raw code expresses in the completest form.

§

In simplicity is strength; in curiosity is action; in learning is enjoyment; in a smile is joy; in a cry a consolation; a child's life is this—plain and simple, yet remarkably colorful and majestic , time immemorial, a psalm of life, a text of nature, an objectivity of science, and the richness of art; all condensed and crystallized in one form, in that little soul, seen in every culture, in every land, highlighting a oneness seldom seen, of a single species, of one race—now say what you will on nationalism.

INTRODUCTION TO CHAPTER 2

Nature: The brilliance, the radiance, the ferocity, the gentleness, the tenacity, the force, the magnificence, the will—all in all every aspect of human life, of human behavior somehow derives from nature. There is much to see, lots to learn from this force we call nature—if there is ever a book that can illustrate the art, or describe the depth of such a thing—called nature—can we do any justice to describe this vital force? To me to even come close to describing such a thing is daunting, for nature is so great in herself that everything else appears small; we can watch, we can learn, we can set off to unravel her riddles, her mysteries . . . in essence everything this world has to show. But every discovery on which we stumble, or each invention that we proclaim, relies on her fundament, her bedrock, her principles, which follow her own laws. I remember a saying I read somewhere about the poet William Wordsworth, when someone asked where he studied to come up with his timeless verses. It said, "This is his library. But his study is out the doors." How apt? How true? Every lover of nature will find meaning in such a comprehension. Let us celebrate nature, preserve her creation, enjoy her works in this short span called life—with this I begin, humbly, yet spirited, my quest in these lines—to *mother* nature, to her I speak, for her I say—a few words.

CHAPTER 2

On Nature

Nature instills in all parents a spark of her own strength; however, this strength has its inverse—the same strength portrays its side, in a mirror, like a coin, and it brings out an unforeseen weakness whenever any adversity befalls their children. How deceiving, when I see happiness on my child's face I find the world colorful, and turn it around, any pain that my child has to face weakens me so much that the same colorful world becomes suddenly devoid of color. Yet this fate that I endure for a day or a week, or a month, is so *pale*—I wonder—in comparison to what nature *must*—for she must see what perhaps no one else can ever bear to see, not just for a brief lapse of time but for all eternity—she must see the whole cycle: she must see the joy of the beginning of a new life at one moment, and the sadness of the ending of some other at the very next—all of whom she births as her very own.

§

Anything magnificent needs a comprehension, for in every magnificent creation lives a grand animation—a thought is merely the means to reflect on the beauty and vigor of such a thing; look at a wonderful sunset or the pristine sunrise, even the half crescent moon picturesque in a dark sky, or the thousand stars that shine to make a sense of the dark . . . yet so far away; it's nature, in her work is magnificence, an endless source of any comprehension. Nature lays out her book—to dwell, marvel, or study what truly is and what will forever remain—her unmatched magnificence.

§

Nature equips every child with extraordinary resilience. I am amazed at her creation, a tiny cell blossoms into a full-blooded life. This adventure must be great in itself, for this journey illustrates nature's work in action, her microscopic detail, a work that remains in my eyes one of immense complexity and staggering brilliance; as soon as a new life breathes we see this in action, how it strives, survives, to tell its tale; it's a common phenomenon, repeated and perfected over thousands of years, yet in every instance of this we can see a novelty, a newness; a child's touch is sublime, his glance heavenly—what can I say other than to watch in awe at this marvelous creation—treat it as sacred, for in each of those souls lives the forces of nature in their most pure and clean form.

§

The heart is a work of nature from the beginning to the end; the structure of the heart is formed even before the head starts to grow; the beats have acquired a rhythm, follow an order, and even perfect a sequence way earlier than the child makes its way into this world. The head on the other hand becomes a product of this world, how it shall work is dictated by the laws and lessons it encounters—disguised as opportunity or reason; nature builds the blocks and then she defers them to what we might say—the hand of fate—for them to take their shape or form. But *heart*, that remains hers, for she is its maker, not just in form but so in its spirit; from where springs all of life's vitality, its vigor—the flashes of inspiration, the moments of rapture, or even for that matter the lone lingering mood. Each of them is perhaps nature's whisper, a reminder to each and every one of us of what she instills—something we often overlook—or simply her way of holding our hand as we face the undeniable will of fate.

§

Every feeling of happiness, every celebration of victory, every excitement of a journey, and even every moment of joy comes to an end in due course. These rules apply to one and all, to every life, as history repeats, civilizations rise and fall, species come and go, to make way for what is new in form but carries much the same in spirit—the spirit of nature herself. The comfort, the sensitivity, and the seriousness that we feel when we are in the lap of nature is perhaps an expression of the intimate awareness that she has, the knowledge of the fact that in the end she must take back from every life what she had so willingly lent—her spirited breath. Every pensive feeling that comes to us of its own will and command reflects nature's deep and serious mood, a truth she valiantly lives with, and one that always ends up seen in her work, no matter how cleverly she tries to hide.

§

Nature reminds me from time to time about the fallacy of our invincibility. She sweeps from under our feet the lunatic fallacy—the pride of our knowledge. The weakest suffer, it appears cruel, when such a thing happens—when a disease spreads around the world creating havoc, pain, misery, suffering. I wonder where did her gentleness go: How could she allow such a thing? Did she transform or was she possessed? Was she helpless or simply stubborn? Nature the wisest of all, the most powerful of all, even the most beautiful of all, must have her say, for she has lent us a free hand, what we call our imagination, and if we dare to disrupt her order, over time she will strike; she will reign with all her rage; the tender hand will become an iron fist and unleash the power of its full force—her unforgiving wrath.

§

The arrival of spring counters the cold of winter; many trees look alike; some exhibit a similar theme, dry branches with no leaves, no scent of a flowering bud; I see them and can sense a different time; each of these trees speaks of a tale, it has survived—and it's in their survival I see a hope, a will, which shall soon show its magic, when leaves bode, flowers bloom, and spring blesses my sore limbs. Yes . . . every face will cheer, every hand shall stay clear, but spare a thought my friends to every tree that stood firm, held its guard, or even perished on its way, against the treacherous cold, the grueling winter; all this so we can witness a new beginning that births a new hope—the wishful spring.

§

Look at a sunset. There is a shining glow around the setting sun, a yellowish golden color; it's bright, pure like a 24-karat gold; now look a little above the horizon—you will see colors, and although they are not as shining and bright as the ones below, they stand out; these colors give the sunset its grandness, its majesty, its appeal; every time the eyes see the heart stirs; the further the light scatters, the more beautiful the color becomes, it stands a chance to create an effect, a freedom perhaps, an urge to get away from the confines of the hot core.

§

A glowing moon in full looks sublime in the night; even a cloud cover does not spoil its beauty, dampen its effect; on the contrary it enhances it; a gathering of clouds scattered around the moon gives the moon a dusky glow; there is tranquility in this view, a consolation around it; it is perfect and artistic just as it is, the clouds radiate the light reflected from the moon, the moon borrows this light from the giant sun; this is nature, her repertoire—where one source *feeds* another, one greatness *inspires* a new one, a beauty preserved, a promise kept, a work cherished for every species to marvel and see.

§

The clouds scatter in precise arrangement, the moon begins its ascent; the night begins in my half of the globe whereas in the other half the day begins; some wake early to see the rising sun, others wrap up to witness its counterpart—the sunset. Each is a spectacle, in each lives a hope, a work of art—you don't need to go really far to see a marvel, you need to wait, each day, each night, climb up a hill, or perhaps look out the window, the Earth and the Sun will align; a celestial event will happen, just like an eclipse but far more common, at the end of every day, the turn of every night, a marvelous, rich, vibrant spectacle—in that hour let us sit back and enjoy the show, for nature will speak of her heavenly glow—be it in the beautiful sunrise or the grand sunset.

§

The sun sets in the clouds, it vanishes from a world that my eyes see; yet in these moments I feel a hope. It's as if this parting carries a message; in it lives a work, a work that shines even after the sun is gone; this *final* hour to me is the *finest*, a culmination of all that came before, a foretaste of all that is yet to come for the world to see. It's at this time we shall see a radiant sky, a beautiful canvas, in which will come to life a colorful masterpiece; the sky will light up, a battle will commence, as every flame shall fight the dark, as every particle of light shall give all its might to fight the darkness that will soon reign the day to become what we call a night. The universe is filled with darkness, yet in it lives a source of light—the sun; the sun stands alone, a lone star, aloof to a point, yet it works to end the dark that surrounds it, it lives to birth light, it shines whether anyone sees or cares and casts its rays far and wide—neither resting, nor ceasing. Science can tell me everything about the sun, but I say the sun hints at so much more; the sun speaks of a never-ending fight, of a hope, of an inexhaustible source of bright, and even if in the end the sun has to die, it lights the dark while it lives—an inspiration to draw from, a spectacle to applaud, and a teaching to remember.

§

A walk relieves an idle mind; the monotony in a walk is a novelty for the mind—a surprising result but a pleasant one; the lungs, the limbs work at the same pace to get this result as the mind races to escape. There are those who walk only when they have some company to engage, and there are others who enjoy their walk only when they walk alone. The latter illustrates an introversion, the former the opposite—extroversion. Yet for all the reasons people walk, we can see a unison of sorts in this art of walking—the limbs, the hands, the heart, and the head come together to achieve an aim or to simply wander in a world that a walk creates—the world of our own imagination.

§

A walk brings a hope, a calm. Some call it a stroll, others a form of exercise, I simply call it a walk. I refuse to search for an advantage in it, or seek to profit from it; it would be like working for a motive rather than to the service to the work itself; walking should be as natural as breathing—a necessity rather than a choice, meant to enjoy, prone to habit. Even an aimless walk is thousand times better I say when there is nothing to do, simply walk; it will bring you things rarely apprehended by the work of deliberation or calculation. Every walk speaks for itself, it reflects the mood, projects the state; there is a temper in it, a class to its gait; and while we can enjoy a walk with a dear friend or a pleasant acquaintance, the one we do alone, in solitude, is the one we do for ourselves; every such walk reminds me of the rules of life—we live our day to our own, sleep our own, just like in the end we must find the strength to breathe our own.

§

I walk. I walk a lot. Sometimes for miles, for hours, in the woods or near a creek; even sometimes on a tar road, cemented path; I walk so I can write; I write because I have something to say, it feels as if words need an expression, like a note needs a melody; somehow my walking is a precursor to my thinking, a walk is a pre-requisite for a thought; there is magic in this simple activity, a complex chain of events sets in when we walk; I do not know any thinker who does not walk; and even if the converse is true, that there may be thinkers who do not walk, for me the finest demonstration this craft of walking and thinking comes from a little child, one who has just learnt to walk; he walks to no end, as if he wishes to touch, feel, sense a piece of every land his feet touch; and when I see him doing in bounds what I do every day, I know I am doing the right thing, for he is a little wonder, a wonder I follow—one whose hand is held by nature, and whose feet by our very own—this Mother Earth.

§

I drive to the shore. The day has been long, bright, the sky clear as I await the beautiful view of the setting sun. To my surprise my wish does not live up, the sun sets without a stir; it's as if I am deprived of a hope, one I had cherished well before the crack of the dawn. What happened? Did someone play a mischief? Science tells me the cause—it is in the arrangement of the molecules, their scatter was blown up by a benign cloud cover, so it says, but today I am not interested in the reason; I am looking for a reason behind the reason; was it my wish that ruined my show? Or someone else's? If it would be raining I can perfectly console myself from such a quandary . . . but it's not—it's bright as summer, golden as it can be, the perfect conditions for a grand exit. Yet the show does not live up. Thousands like me must have waited the same way I did, or even the few who stand next to me are feeling the same I feel—a little disappointed, a little robbed. Is this a game of Fate? You wish something and you get the opposite. The curse of a wish. Alas this reminds me of something—Life. Life is a little of this, every hope, every aspiration, takes its time, runs its course; so even if the head *frets* every so often, the heart still *beats*; it *beats* to every jubilation, to every disappointment, to each day, to each night, until so; *like a star it lives and hence so shall I*; there is not much to worry, nor to deject, for even the most humble of asks take their own sweet time—let alone the grand sunset.

§

I see euphoria. I see everyone ferry in excitement from one place to another. I see lights put up on a curved lane to celebrate the festivals of winter. It's lovely and beautiful in December in the town I live in! The best of ideas come to life in the cold of this month; art is in full form, music in full flow; turn on the radio to carols galore; a bookstore or an art shop comes to life in this month, the month of winter solstice, when the rays are shallow, dispersed, and scattered; yet there is unity, assembly, and togetherness during this time, in the alleys, in the shops, in the music, even in the candles or the lamps—it's as if every house takes its guard and announces in a firm voice—o dear winter. Come and see me. I await your arrival. And don't you worry, for even if you bring all the cold at my door, I stand here to welcome you with all my warmth.

§

The fall colors are a pleasure to the eye; it's colorful near my home; each tree stands in a file bearing leaves; the leaves exhibit a beautiful color, a soft texture, an inviting touch; some of these leaves are of the same type, others completely varied; walk a few steps and the color changes from a bright yellow to a crimson orange; it's perfectly crafted, I ask nothing more; the walk brings a smile to my face and to anyone who can pause a little; as I look up my eyes see ornaments of gold; certainly appears so—in the color, the layout, the arrangement of the branches and its leaves; my eyes are locked, head still—*heaven in a few square feet*—I wonder; soon winter will arrive and these trees will wither—is this their finest hour, I ask? Only as they near their end their work shines the most? Is this a rule of nature, or even of life? The best speaks the last, waits its turn; even the setting sun hints the same; it's just before the dark when the sky lights up in all its color, just like these trees that light up my alley before the onset of winter.

§

This lockdown haunts my head, the quarantine prisons my heart; the things in my home fail to uplift my mood, at this point I wonder—every possession pales in comparison to the necessity of freedom, the need to step out, the need to feel the breeze, the need of the spirited breath; this need to be free is rooted in each one of us, the need to be in the midst of the hills, the valleys, the forests, the oceans—in essence the comforting lap of nature.

§

The will of a disease—a curse to one, a vice to many. Every century witnesses it, every history book narrates a form of it. An episode of a monstrous disease reveals the fragility of life. Life, the gentle, the tender creation of nature is brought to its knees by a product of nature herself; it is she, the wisest, the revered, the most beautiful of all, who unleashes all her wrath on the children who are her very own. Is she helpless or has she become merciless, devoid of care, blind to compassion? I do not know what to say other than to face her fury, resign to the will of this disease—a disease that propagates through the very fabric of her creation. But in this darkest hour my will speaks; it leaps, it rises, it aspires, and confronts my fear; I shall fight, I shall prevail, and even if in the end I must perish . . . I shall not without airing my might; even the dark sky has a thousand lights, so shall my last breath; let her also see in my parting moment the strength of my will, the will that is really her very own, the will she instills, the will she lends, the will of my first breath—in essence the will of life.

§

The spread of a disease is perhaps the worst spread of a kind, it spreads not to a person, but to the society as a whole—bringing in pain, fear, anxiety, isolation, and in the end panic. It kills a life and does not stop there—it robs every life around it of its living. Nature's wrath—shall we say, or our own foolishness compounded over time—in either case we can see the fragility of our existence, compared to the multiplicative laws of nature. Set them in action and you can see a cascade, like the dominoes falling off a cliff with the touch of a little hand. Nevertheless, the fight goes on—human resolve persists, rises, and unites in every such fight. There is much to fear, or there may not be much left to fight, yet I see a light in every such fight, for what good is life that fails to fight, if in the end it has to perish without a show of its might?

§

The good times appear scarce and scanty—before they can be relished fully they simply disappear—any calamity of nature cripples it, invades the pleasing, the gentle. The transitory nature of a happy moment is evident, it feels so weak compared to the permanence of an unpleasant one; it's as if there is no chance to stand against this merciless unknown. The ghosts of the night are felt, the fragility of being a human is seen. To whom can we pray? No one but ourselves, for we have to fulfill our own destiny in the company of those hands that shatter it.

§

Fear . . . the word is enough to make the world spin around, trade halt, people panic, and cultures collide when fear reigns and rules. Look at a new life who just made its way into this world, I can claim with his first breath there is a show of fear; the way he cries, the way it's necessary for him to cry, for his lungs to pump the air into his brain, so he can live, is for all we know—a response to fear. Fear demands a response, a vociferous one, sometimes even a violent one; to confront fear is nature's teaching, just like a new life shows—the infant is bare, screams naked, and he fights to prevail, so he can live, so then why shouldn't we with all our cloth and armor—for we did it then so why can't we do it now?

§

Dreams—a wonder of the mind. Try taking a walk on a breezy day next to an ocean, climbing up a hill, and let your mind wander. Aspirations will speak, hopes will rise, puncturing the dreariness, the dullness of the day so a colorful canvas brightens the slate—the slate of the mind. This is rightly daydreaming, yet sometimes a wonderful elevation, an escape, a transportation to a world that appears within one's grasp, within one's sight of a pending achievement. I can't think of any other activity for leisure than such a one, of walking and thinking, for if I have to finish writing a thought, I need to dream, I need to let my mind wander, so it can speak of its own free will, since after all it may be nature's voice or her whisper, to which I shall listen no matter how far-fetched it may seem and however impossible it may be.

§

The sun sets. Another day goes by. Life for me is much the same. Nothing changes insofar as before. Yet my mind does not quieten. Curiosity keeps me alive, but on some days even curiosity is not enough; something in the air gets the better of me. The only remedy then is an aimless walk, not to sit still but to be out, in the woods, in the company of nature—the hope being . . . the walk shall lead the day. I wonder if life is the same for a bee, a spider, or an ant. They don't seem to have much of a choice in every act they do, yet they live each day busy, occupied, and engrossed. They do not meditate or chant hymns yet they live in a manner perhaps the way nature wishes, how she envisions them to live. *They strive to perfect the tasks at hand.* Even among us humans, children exhibit this behavior, a raw will possesses them; they will their own, imagine their own, play their own; it's only later when the world sings its tune and we participate in its choir, we see things, we hear people—the dubious, the deceitful, the delusional; some preach stillness, others a false hope; their practices offer a cure, so they claim, but I feel this is simply an indulgence—a fancy, a fantasy, a farce. My mind finds this to be plain gibberish, my heart says this is a salesman selling hope; for what good is life with our eyes closed, head still, and mind vacant—likened to a stone? They ask me to look within, but I say look far, see the world; for me stillness is illness, meditation a half cure; even nature casts her works far and wide; she does it in thousands what our eyes see only a few; she repeats a sequence—seasons or life—at every onset; there is not much new in each season, or each day within it, so why should it be in everyday life? Yet when it comes to life, people preach to deceive otherwise; they seek to sell the old as new, the stale as fresh, but life at its core remains the same; even nature for all her magnificence hints the same; she repeats and perfects what she has done ever since—*her tasks at hand*; so why shouldn't we, for we are one of hers and she one among us all?

§

What a world this must be; a look up to a clear night sky will convey what I mean; the million stars decking it, the comets circling those stars, the auroras giving it color, it's awe inspiring and majestic; a glimpse of the heavens from the narrow sphere of the eye. This world with all the suns and the moons are like a work of art; the constellations, the galaxies, are so vast apart, so far away that we may never reach them; yet our minds imagine them, picture them, construct them, and even study them; there is a wonder in the universe in which we live, and while its vastness gives it the grandness, there is another universe that is rarely spoken, rarely felt, and even rarely seen; it's one that is in every life, a wonder that makes me a me and you a you, a universe within our own selves—a universe within the magical mind.

§

What a piece of work these honeybees create. A thousand bees live together for a short time, each having even a shorter life span; this honey is their work—one that has been used for a multitude of things; kings, queens use it in their coronation; priests consider it sacred; doctors recommend it as a medicine; some claim it to be fertile, others believe it to be auspicious. I am stumped, amazed at what these bees do; these swamp of bees, an inch in length and a few centimeters in height, come together to work so they can leave a mark—through their work, work alone . . . the creation of honey. I hail their triumphs; I cannot think of anything organic that can last so long; this work of theirs is imperishable, immortal if preserved with a little help; it lasts decades, generations, centuries, in essence forever. Quite rightly it possesses a color of gold; timeless, I say—what a species!

§

A honeybee's life is simple. It has a task to do, one task, maybe two, which it perfects in the short life it lives. There is an order in its life, no confusion, no reason, only execution. The honeybee is like a well-programmed robot that knows precisely from the time it is born exactly what it needs to do—the asks, the activities, the demands, are all weaved in its genetic code. It does not try to perfect many things, just one, confines itself to a single home, and gives its life for its whole family—the honeycomb. What a service, we should grant every honeybee a medal, a star, for it lives a life within its means and in a manner befitting its purpose. Every honeybee is perfect insofar as it is, a gifted life I say, that faithfully and fearlessly obeys and serves one master—nature—who is its teacher from its early start and remains so till its very end.

§

There are so many things our eyes have yet to see; bring a catalogue of the world and you will see what is left to see; even after you travel the whole world, walk through all the alleys, sit near the ponds, the beaches, sail across the lakes, the oceans, yet on a homecoming there is something new; take a peek around your backyard, or walk through your front yard, there will be a new specimen that has grown, perhaps a weed, a flower, a patch of soil by the change of season, a freshness, a uniqueness of nature. So is a mind—the more you tinker the more it grows, it challenges you more, so am I to say the finest minds I know are the finest minds there are; there are plenty I believe, who live unnoticed . . . away from the glaring eye. This reminds me of the neglected flower in the garden, but a flower nonetheless, the friends we tend to, friends we say we plan to tend to . . . yet who we forget—like the plant in the corner of my backyard that lives without any fuss. I say tend to such, attend a friend, or a company; a plant is nourished and nurtured on the soil it grows in first and foremost, well before anyone can see and notice—let alone an expert of nature.

§

The scorching sun rests, the wind leaps and dries the sweat of my face, the clouds draw a curtain to put on a show; suddenly the day is less bright, less hot, yet there is light, a certain peace, a quiet, as I watch the gentleness of nature come into play—in the trees, the leaves, the branches, the twigs, or for that matter the sordid rock that has forever lain in my plain sight. Time and again these events unfold in every season of the year, allowing me to conjure, to reflect on what is more, what is dear—on a light within, a light that lives in my heart, a light of nature, a light that glows even as the light of the whole world dims allowing me to see what I have always looked for, but simply failed to see.

§

The rain stops, the clouds nudge, the sun shines, the rays penetrate to reach the surface, and behold we have a rainbow—in minutes this rainbow vanishes, the spectacle gone, the show over, as I stare at the empty sky; someone asked where did the rainbow go? In the heavens, I say, for there it is born and hence there it shall perish.

§

A mishap or a misfortune exposes the sensitivity of life; the hardness of nature reveals a softness of a kind; grief is painful, sorrow unbearable, yet tears speak of a softness, a language I say is apprehended by our senses, comprehended by the heart; nature reminds me of the perenniality of these, and through it the commonality of each, for every life in the end has had a story to tell, a tear that it has shed, and an episode on which it has wept.

§

A turbulent ocean puts on a show, the waves roar, they appear as tiny specks of white far and away, like the thousand lights on a clear night sky, all seen with the naked eye; in them is a force so strong, it pulls and pushes everything that comes in the way, how mighty is this force, measure the speed of the wind, feel its howl and one can dwell; even the birds that enjoy the dance of the waves disappear, beaches are empty, people flounder to the safety of their homes—a rage runs within the ocean and the ocean dances with a roar telling everyone near his abode—let me be me who I am, so that you can enjoy me from a distance as much as you can.

§

The waves treat the eyes to a simple yet a sublime show; the breeze kisses the ears and renders a pulse; a pulse on which the heart leaps and the head rests to fathom the enormity of this majestic creation, a place where the wind runs free as the waves soar high, a dance to freedom perhaps—by the ocean himself.

§

The oceanic shore stands for magnificence, its vastness and its size. Every human settlement that stands on the shores of these seas salutes in awe, and respect, a submission to what the ocean brings and what the ocean has—his depth.

§

The beauty of a small town next to the vast ocean is one of a kind; a juncture between the old and the new, the timeless and the transient, a blend between a marvel of nature and the masterful work of a man. Centuries pass by, the town changes in size, shape, and form, yet the ocean stands, watches, witnesses, and transforms every human dwelling into a picturesque abode, thus offering every stranger his respite, his rest, his solitude, and perhaps even his solace.

§

The waves that reach the shores have a uniform pattern, yet they hold the attention of the eye as well as the ear in perfect synchrony. It feels as if these waves want to convey a message when they conduct a dance with each other while nearing their end, thus transforming what looks still, to that which has movement. Perhaps, this is the ocean's way of telling us something, that in his enormity, in his vastness, in his might or even in his rage, lies a heart of a tender artist, which he shows by this dance he orchestrates, a dance that never stops, allowing us to enjoy his show whenever we visit the shore.

§

The ocean plays music, he brings to the ears a tune, a tune of action, a tune with movement, a tune distinctly his own, a tune hinting on the qualities of life itself, of the vastness and depth that there is, a tune of continuity, a tune illustrating in its own way the repetition and recitation of a script of nature, on how she repeats for every life a sequence, which for all its differences remains a recital of the same theme.

§

The ocean spreads far and wide yet harbors the tiniest of life ever known to man. It may appear insignificant in the midst of our aims or our aspirations, but it does highlight one thing: Every life is granted a chance by nature, a place where her many forms rule and govern, flourish and prosper, grow and multiply, to call it their home—this Mother Earth. Yet nature's most daring hope, her meticulous creation, perhaps human life itself, fails to grasp her lesson, when a man uses all his reason to justify his greed, so he can take from her all that she willingly gives, to ruin what is rightfully hers, to become what she silently dreads—devilish and demonic.

§

The wind gets a free pass in the vastness of the ocean; the waves stage a show to express their delight; and the ocean speaks in a majestic tone the qualities he possesses—his size and his depth. The heart finds the spirit of adventure in his size and the head the range of imagination in his depth.

§

The oceanic waves have a calming feel; there is hardly any variation in the overall rhythm, slight if any, yet in their simplicity is a depth, like that felt in a musical synchrony. This feeling has no relation to the ocean's size, for even in the darkness of the night when there is not much to see, we listen to the tone even if the tune is much the same. It illustrates a principle worth remembering that an effect can arise only from the object that possesses it, be it in any human or nature, just like the ocean, for what the ocean has, he reflects—his depth.

§

Such grand magnificence meets the eye, when the towering mountains stand next to the vast ocean, as the sun goes down transforming the clear blue sky into a colorful canvas, while the moon slowly peeks out of its hiding, and as the waves adorn themselves with what appear as tiny specks of gold, all done as if to celebrate an occasion, the hour when day meets the night, is perhaps only a glimpse of nature's many unique and beautiful worlds, all a part of her rich and varied repertoire. It is she, who can offer every life a certain comfort, a loner a company, an artist an inspiration, a writer the material, the mind an imagination, and while she does all of this, she still preserves the purity and essence of her work by hiding some of it, earthly or celestial, from every man's sight. We may never find out about the thousand worlds she creates, but then that is man in power for you, on how he robs, plunders, and spoils every new land he sets his foot on, so he can reign and govern the very land that was never rightfully his.

§

The vastness of the ocean has its own charm; all that we see is one and the same, yet its size holds our gaze for as far as we can see and for how long we may wish. The effect of the clear night sky is much the same, when the heavens open up to show a tiny fraction of their size, the numerous worlds with their million suns all tucked in their own Milky Ways, making us wonder of our place in this cosmos. While both of them—the earthly and the celestial—are different in form, they remain similar in class, as they bring out in life a pioneering spirit, an appeal, an urge to explore, so much so that every pursuit becomes an adventure, an eternal quest, be that of solving the mystery of the heavens or that of discovering new lands.

§

The ocean's spirit resonates vividly in his waves more than in his size. While his size is a clear symbol of his might, the waves speak of his class on how he ensures that life survives, multiplies, and prevails by allowing, aiding, and abetting her rich and numerous forms to reach the many lands his waves visit.

§

The waves come to an end in the sands after a long journey, and even if their unison ends as the eye blinks, a new cycle repeats, with the new set replenishing the old one, for long and eternal.

§

The ocean's vastness is a symbol of his might, on how he reigns supreme by the many forms he so expresses, from a serene calm to a turbulent rage, with a range that goes beyond what the eyes can see or even what the mind can imagine. Yet in all his glory, he remains incomplete without the Earth, as he needs her, the consent of her will, so that he can show the world his greatness, with the vital and the vigorous force scattered from his nucleus. And while the Earth affords all that she wills, allowing life to rule and govern her many lands, carrying the scars, the remains of all the life she bears, and granting every species a chance to flourish and prosper, but in the end, her powers fall a little short as she needs the ocean, as without him she would harbor no life, becoming a dry and a parched rock with no soul present to enjoy. Quite rightfully, the two of them possess celestial beauty when blended together, which even the heavens and their Gods will notice, for in them lies a trace of the valiant attempt on how life and her many forms lived and breathed in this cycle of time.

§

The ocean dissolves every boundary a nation claims on paper; life is free to roam its waters, just as free the wind is when it blows; what a wonderful sight it must be for anyone to see from the gallery of the heavens the mighty ocean as one single mass, a contiguous block, and to know that life finds a home, prevails, and flourishes in the oneness of the ocean, in spite of all that a man does by his conquests and divisions in the name of nationalism.

§

The ocean compels the mind into a state of complete submission yet harboring a feeling of inspiration. This effect is almost automatic where the sheer size of the ocean gives a humbling feel, yet pushes the mind to open those doors that can foray into the future or reflect on the past. The sounds arising from the waves that reach the shore are a treat for the ears, winds a scent of freshness for the breath, and a view a chance for the eyes to see the enormity that stands right in front of us. And even if the ocean's size puts a limit on how far we can see, it does not impose any limit on the reach of human thought; on the contrary, through its vastness the ocean offers a compensation, a chance for the mind to awaken the powers of unlimited imagination.

§

Dance is an expression of life. It illustrates at its core a principle imbibed in every animated life form—that of action and movement. Every human life in its infancy portrays this animation to the fullest; the movement of the hands, the swivel of the face, the roll of the eyes, or the tap of the feet is natural as a breath; in fact when the child learns to stand, the first thing he does is signals how much he loves this act, and then in a more artistic and opulent form, by a primitive dance. Every culture has one, every civilization witnesses many, and even every creation of nature brings out this form—be that in the waves of the ocean, the swaying of the branches, or the howl of the wind. What is it? It is a dance, a show put on by nature herself to remind each and every one of us of how she is and what she has—the force of her action and movement.

§

The first indication of a life is in a heartbeat; the first demonstration of intelligence springs in a thought; the heart's rhythm is common to all, while the head's strife is the onus of one. Night or day the heart does the same, beats to a rhythm, a monotonic wave; a waveform that supplies not just the brain its magical potion, one responsible for its intelligence, its intellect but holds the pulse of life itself. The head on the other hand becomes opportunistic, strives to govern and reign. The world rules over one while nature whispers to the other . . . who shall win?—the heart who beats to the tune of nature or the head who bows to the hand of fate.

§

The greatness of life is not in its form, but in the class; man has progressed, he has contested and conquered, set his foot on every land this Earth has to show, even the skies are within his reach, the secrets hidden in them are a challenge to his insatiable mind; his every achievement is full of pride and all his aspirations emblem a posture, of a superiority, of a might perhaps none of the other species possess—but then why when the same man becomes a father to his own child, his own flesh and blood so to speak, all his contests and conquests vanish, disappear, in front of this little life; the child comes along, and with a single glance shows him what is real, what makes life shall I say worth living, makes him forget what this world sings or asks; he sees art, he feels nature in the child itself; this little life reflects a lofty class, a class that every life possesses, and one that every life derives only from a superhuman source—the kernel of nature herself.

§

The innate spirit of nature is at its best in those formative and nimble years; nothing disappoints enough, no adulation or praise has much effect; we live to learn, and learn we do; the hands we hold, the arms we sit in, or the shoulders we rest on are prized over anything else that this world shows; the world with its thousand chimeras fails in its persuasion to sway us away; the soul remains intact, the spirit vibrates, speaks and allows life to grow; but come much later the situation is reversed; we miss, cry, or shake at the slightest grudge, a fall, or a setback; it's as if life has resigned a part of itself to this world, the exact opposite of what a child does—the child in us who was then the child in full gave life all the space it needed more than this world would ever have . . . perhaps highlighting the secret on living, one that we often see on the face of a young child time and again, in spite of all the adversities or misfortunes that child may face. This is the text on living, the secret on how to live, a universal text of every life yet a unique composition for each one, accessible we might say only to that life itself, a text that no one can ever teach and a text that no one fully knows.

§

Life never waits, living does not stop, the moments we experience never come back; they pass by our eyes in a flash, well before we can comprehend the sweetness they have, or the warmth they can bring; the life of every such moment is finite, it lives for a brief time—a few seconds perhaps, before it vanishes from our consciousness, yet in that brief span, it leaves a mark, an indelible impression, delivering a heartfelt effect each time we reminisce—of an inspiration, of enrichment, or even of a consolation; here we see the genius of nature in all its color and shade, how she creates a storehouse where every such moment rests, so it can be retrieved time and again, from the very depths of our nerve and tissue—a work of the remarkable complexity, astonishing detail, in essence a work of genius—the magical mind.

§

How mighty and marvelous this nature must be, as her laws pervade throughout this world and percolate in every species, the animate and the inanimate are bound by them; the vibrancy of the animate contrasts with the variety of the inanimate, each has a marked distinction, a clear pattern, a definite purpose, becoming a specimen for a study; every understanding of a law hints at a different one, yet a beautiful one in itself; it speaks of nature's vast vocabulary, her rich repertoire, perhaps a glimpse of her world; how fortunate it is that this very young human race can dwell, reflect, or even linger on these marvelous creations, learn from them, and perhaps adapt to them, to see how they are, what they consist of; from mathematics to music, all fields of the sciences or the arts strive to prove what is and remains essentially hers—the ideas themselves.

§

The repetition of all inanimate and animate objects of nature—of her work—remains a source of consolation to the short span of life. Almost every phenomenon that begins . . . ends, it follows the rules and decree of some higher order, a necessity to which each of us bows and one to which each of us follows. Even the mighty sun with its power to brighten the world has a span, he lightens up the planets that come in his path and to some who are blessed nature's most remarkable and magnificent creation dwells—life itself. This ounce of life that every species breathes and lives is a compelling demonstration of the temporariness of every phenomenon, yet illustrates the permanence of nature's spirit, which happens to leave its mark in all the things this world has, be that the mighty sun or a minuscule life—it is and remains nature's way to exhibit all that she must in this wrap of time.

§

A man may be one of nature's most daring creations, but it is the woman who fully expresses her complexity, mirrors her nurture, or even reflects her class; for only a woman does to life what nature does to the world; she grows one, lends it her breath, nourishes it with her own lifeblood, and then brings it into the world for everyone to see.

§

Perfection is always a joy to watch; it is the art of concealing the complexity of the craft yet being adept in it; the inner workings vanish in the expression of the art or the activity itself, yet they allow themselves to be comprehended by those who dwell; this is an adage of nature. Who are we to question it? Her many forms that end up pleasing the eye do so not because they are simple but because they are expressed so; it is an apt demonstration of her mastery and speaks of an invaluable lesson in excellence—the fruits of labor are seen only in a life of toil, in the countless hours of repetition imbibed in a lifetime of practice.

§

Nature has arranged everything within us precisely so we function as a whole; we perfect a necessary craft, a continuous activity simply by imitation and practice; in short, breathing, walking, talking, hearing, seeing, and countless things that we all do are taken care of without any conscious exertion, it's like all that we must learn is already known deep in our hearts, nature ensures this happens in the course of our life. However, some things nature has chosen to omit, she has left it out for us to dwell; to think on the imperfect and the unknown, the vast and the tiny, the hundreds and thousands of riddles and mysteries this world has, the answers we all seek, only possible because she has given us all a wonderful gift, perhaps her finest, the seat of our intelligence—our beautiful mind.

§

There is order and timeliness in every work of nature. It's a hallmark of her style, a glimpse of her class, as she does all that she must without ever falling behind—right from governing the motion of the stars, to the supervision of life well before its birth. Nothing gets past her; her steady hand is felt even if not seen; every monumental achievement in understanding more of nature happens because the text for such a comprehension comes from nature herself. It's as if when we unravel some of her secrets she reveals a few more, thus giving us a consolation in the brief span we live that there is lots to learn, more to see—her text as the source of all the knowledge that there is, and her text being the script of her own show, a show this world sees, a show of staggering proportions—a show that simply goes on.

§

Genius lives and works in nature. It's not the complexity of her work that gives it the tag of a genius, but the expression of it, on how she abstracts her inner workings from everyone so it can be universally enjoyed yet individually followed, allowing every keen mind to dwell on the detail and the comprehension that there is.

§

If nature is a living soul, her text must be music; for both in themselves are heavenly and divine, are dazzling and magnificent; they remain of such class and distinction, rank and stature that they are well beyond any match, above any comparison; hence every idea that comes to us whenever we are in their company is heartfelt and genuine; it's as if nature portrays the ideas that this world has, while music expresses each one of them showing how this world is.

§

This world shows us how different each of us is, but nature illustrates how similar each one of us remains; for every work of hers at once finds an audience as she lays out everything for everyone to see. It's as if we are ridden of our biases, our prejudices when we are in the company of nature to see the idea as it needs to be seen. From this it follows that brilliance is the replay of her ideas that our heart needs, or a comprehension of her details that our head wants, but the original is and shall remain hers.

§

Every work of nature speaks of her class, her style, and even her grace; she repeats and replenishes everything this world sees, while hiding from everyone the pain beneath her smile and the tears behind her laugh.

§

A beautiful sunset lays out in front of our eyes a world of art, a world we long to be; the vivid colors seen during the hour are perhaps the finest our eyes can ever see; this cusp where the day makes way for the night is a spectacle that remains well beyond the will or command of any life; is one that offers a solace to a hard day, a memory to a jubilant occasion; is an event that happens because it must; and remains one that has in itself a heavenly glow, a quintessential beauty, one that no life can ever touch and hence one which no life can ever spoil.

§

How beautiful and intelligent this nature must be, her force, as she sets off to create from raw dust, or a tiny egg, a life, so complex, of multitudes of forms, in air or water, of speed or distance, whose workings with their thousand intricacies, delicately woven, are a marvel and a delight for any mind to spend his whole life on, yet only to find out that what was accomplished in the end is a mere comprehension of her scribbles from her vast book of knowledge. There is much to learn, there is much to see, but one thing is clear: Her work—animate or inanimate—always speaks of her class, her steady hand, her minute eye, and her imaginative mind—a hallmark of genius be it a thousand years back or a million years hence.

§

Our whole capacity to reason rests on nature's original, be that the doctor who dissects life or the poet who portrays it, what each of them ends up doing is quite similar; they study her, understand her, the many shades therein, the mammoth complexities thereof, which are in themselves a marvel to see from the eyes of human thought.

§

Every arrival of a new life shiningly reflects an idea of nature, a pure, clean object, which she produces a thousand a day for the world to see. Such a life has the glow and shine of a fresh painting, a contemplation of an idea whose richness is perhaps even beyond the capacity of human reason. It may as well be why reason has no place to rule in the years of early childhood, it never finds its way into the child's head, for the child is what he is, a wonder of nature, a work of art, a living idea, a fresh creation, whose depth yet simplicity resembles much of her other work—glowing, radiant, spirited, artistic, pure, clean, all in all a work of genius. Only later when childhood is over and he has assimilated fully in this world, learning the tricks of the trade, becoming well versed in the mimicry and tradecraft that so abounds, does he find the need to go back, in search of what is true and authentic in itself, a place where his heart can rule and his head can rest, like a mother's lap, or more aptly the lap of nature herself.

§

This universe and all things that are in it, if we are to say are the work of Fate, an unavoidable accident, or a meticulous design, then Nature is tasked to govern everything within it, perhaps with a decree of freedom but not beyond the laws of Fate. All things we see, we feel, or we know lie within the bounds of a necessity, the necessity of all existence, not just one life but everything everywhere, inanimate or animate, at all times, all of which must eventually end—including the end of nature herself or more aptly the end of all ends. It may be satisfying to know that this knowledge we are after, or the knowledge of this kernel of truth so to speak, from which everything originates, is perhaps rightfully hidden by nature, for it carries a responsibility far greater than our hands can carry and has a burden far more than our shoulders can bear. And while we can leave that to nature, to her judgement about what she decides to reveal, we can see that our life is one of hers, so if we wish to run her show, we must reflect the exemplary qualities she has and avoid the heinous ones she dreads, in our work or in our deeds, and while doing so never incur her wrath, for she rules and reigns over all that we think is our own—whether it be our land or for that matter even our breath.

§

Every life has a clock with which she has to live by, the tick being the beat of her heart. Nature grants every life, insofar as the species is concerned, the same speed with which a life has to live, as the heart for all we know does not deviate much at every age; it beats within a range; it beats per the will of nature. And this beat that has given us our moment, whether it be of joy or pain, or of dullness or excitement, is ordained and not free, for why else can we grasp the essence of what we have felt—our present moment—only when it has passed and never while it happens?

§

Gold is certainly a metal possessing a natural power as it remains a gift from the heavens—anyone who doubts this can watch the setting sun and the rays beating down on the ocean—there lies the gold, place an ounce of gold next to the waves and see if there is any difference.

§

The cycle of seasons alludes to a principle of living—the inevitability of change and the necessity of repetition that pervades in this world and hence follows through in every walk of life. In this change, which is orchestrated by nature herself, we can find many distinct qualities of her work, on how she manages to retain her charm, her elegance, and her uniqueness in spite of having to do what she has done a thousand times before and what she will do a thousand times again. Even in this repetition is there a class, a fresh scent as the new season approaches, as we stand on the cusp thinking all that she will *bring* and all that she must *take*.

§

The flower of the cereus cactus plant blooms only once a year and that too only for a single night; the flower never lives to see the light of the sun, withering well before the crack of dawn, its whole life away from the watchful eyes of the world, yet it blooms and blossoms while the world sleeps, perhaps a lesson to the world in the brief time that it lives, on how it triumphs with its will alone, its glow being the only aid to fight the dark that permeates through the silence of the night.

§

Every creation by nature has a timeless appeal, is perpetual, and speaks of a conduct about her way of work. The lessons she imparts lie above and beyond the affairs of trade or profit, contain superhuman principles, and hence remain true to their teaching—which each of us must learn and which each of us must follow. While her beauty and her grace are admired a lot, what ends up speaking the most is simply her work. Her work never stops no matter how the world behaves, it lives long even if the world does not care to look, nothing breaks her resolve as she perfects what she herself creates, without a care or a worry, thus showing us what greatness really is and where genius truly lies—only in our will and through it our work.

§

Every object of nature speaks to us in a tender yet a majestic manner; hence we can stare at her creation without much ado—be it the setting sun or the full moon. From this inspiration is bred a genuine thought, the consolation being that behind every such thought in a poem, a painting, a philosophical idea, or even in the work of sciences, lies a mint, a reservoir of ideas, far deeper than what we can imagine and far richer than what we can possess—the genius of nature herself.

§

The growth of life is an astonishing phenomenon. It remains perhaps nature's finest work, of genius and brilliance, on how she can grow from a mere tiny mix, a full life, of vigor and vitality, a complex organism in itself, the process we rarely think of yet whose proceeds we fully enjoy.

§

The order found in nature's work is remarkable; everything happens like a well-kept promise. Seasons change, flowers bloom, comets arrive, planets revolve, and even life follows the course she has set. Yet the vital force that makes all this glue together is a mystery, as perplexing as the question of life itself. The genius of nature lies not so much in the complexity, or her inner workings so to speak, which by far are a challenge to any curious mind to riddle on, but on how she abstracts, absolves, and alienates everyone from her details, from the complexities therein, to bring an order in the chaos, which each of us feels whenever in her company. The job of philosophy is precisely this—to compose the prose of the poem that nature whispers in the ear.

§

Leisure is to the mind what tranquility is to the heart. Whatever we do and wherever we are, the world catches up to us with its asks, a never-ending imposition of this or that, thus shattering a quiet moment into a busy one. Leisure grants us this escape, a road out into our woods, and even if it cannot promise us any happiness, it keeps its word on freedom, from where we can see through the cloth those threads that weave up our life.

§

Nature whispers to every heart and may be the reason why we can feel at ease, close to her, at home, in the simplest of acts, be it a leisurely swim or a carefree walk.

§

It is ironic to see that the woman who dazzled us in her lap or delighted us in her arms—our mother—has to wait her turn when childhood comes to a glorious end. The love, the care, the warmth, the play, or even the kiss that a mother gives to her child, is taken for granted as years go by, like a rule is this seen with every life, almost a necessity of all living. These moments lose their voice when manhood starts to talk, when the world and its wants fill up our ears more than her goodnight hum, or when our aims and aspirations engulf us so much that we walk ahead without realizing that she has long been left behind. Yet in spite of all this, in her worries or in her woes, *there she stands* on a moment's call, ready to guard with all her will what remains her prize, her hope, her cherished past, her love towards what is hers *first*, for which she fights with her every breath even if that breath is to be her very *last*. Such unparalleled love a mother feels for her child is seen in every culture, in every land, and perhaps in every cradle where life has found the care to take its rightful shape and form. It would not be wrong to remark that in all the vanity and wickedness that this world has, we witness something pure and exceptional, one that is human in form but remains superhuman in class, and one that is handed down to a woman by none other than nature herself—an unselfish and unconditional love of what there is and what there can ever be—motherhood.

§

Every work of nature speaks to us tenderly yet truthfully of her form and her material, essentially herself. With no one to stop us, we feel like a prince; we can do what we want, see her, admire her, while she speaks, thus awakening in us what she herself has—genius.

§

Repetition is the hallmark of nature. Every object arising from her substance confirms to this rule. Life is as well a repetition, a phenomenon of her material, pattern after pattern, form after form, species after species, which she evolves and perfects day after day and night after night. Perhaps this gives nature her immeasurable quality of excellence, of resilience, of an invincible strength and an immortal existence—a lesson we mere mortals can earnestly follow in the trade or craft we choose to do, by this habit of practice and repetition in the finite span of our lives.

§

A single stroke of nature; the sky changes color, the trees adorn a color, the dull and dreary routines of the day are put to bed, life within us wakes up, in her arms to attend to her voice. From the mighty cliffs to the splashing waves, we can see her beauty, her wonder, her charm, and in many waves the powers of her creation, in her company we find delight and comfort—who can do it with a single stroke—the genius of nature.

§

The moon borrows the light from the sun and uses it to give us a picture that all of us can stare and reflect. While the setting sun is grand and majestic, the full moon remains sublime and silent thereby giving us a feeling of quiet. The dark spots that it carries come to life with the limited light it uses, reflecting in part the pensive nature in each of us. The sun remains its master and even if the moon in full does not carry the might of the sun, it talks to us in its own way, giving us the hope that there comes a source every now and then, assured by the clock of time that can stand guard against the dark of the night.

§

Nature has endowed our heavenly rock with mighty oceans, majestic falls, vibrant colors, sublime views; this in itself is a wonder of her capacity, one we try to comprehend. Even sitting at the oceanfront and looking at the waves surfing in harmony with each other will give us the power of the underlying force that she uses to make this happen. Why she did this is an open question that every audience can brood and reflect. But surely it will not be hard to contemplate that her service and capacity is not merely meant for the human race, or a privilege just for us, as it can go beyond our comprehension or even our senses. For her such a display may be a frivolous task, and not the final limits of her powers, or her reach—one we are so valiantly after. And whatever the reason for such a creation is, isn't it worthwhile to be thankful to her for it? Life dances to the tune of nature; every feeling in her company is genuine, we consume one to produce another—a summation of her touch moment after moment.

§

The setting sun is a sight almost everyone enjoys to see, even though what follows in due course is darkness. Lights are put up and the moon glows in phases to bring a sense to this dark; to make us merry we gather with others to cheer up the mood. But it is precisely at this merge, the intersection of day and night where we get to see nature, her artwork, in a captivating form, giving some consolation to what is to follow. In that final hour, the sun allows us to look at it directly, granting that wish by making us wage for it till the end of the day. And after his departure we have the leftovers of his work, those rays that remain in the sky. If this work is not genius, where we can pause to view the same story day after day, what is?

§

There is a strange eeriness today, emptiness I say; perhaps it's the room, the temperature, the environment, the coffee maker, or even just the state of things, a thought refuses to come, the mind does not shape a form; yes, I wait for a thought, I do not fish for it but I let it speak of its own will—it's almost unnatural to me to manufacture a thought by reason when I feel the need to write; I do not want to rob it of its purity, its freedom, and while some may disagree, this method grants me a satisfaction of attaining the end without knowing the means, like love without the arithmetic, without the reason behind it; you do not reason it, square it, or integrate it, you simply fall in love or let it sweep you, for if you reason a lot then it's not love, but something else, muddier and impure. A thought can be crafted with reason, polished with reason, elaborated with reason, enriched with reason, even made presentable with reason, but to impregnate it with reason for it to surface is a road I do not wish to take when I pick up my pen—hence most of my days are empty, just like most of the days of nature are the same.

§

Walking enforces a rule, a gait, a motion—it's a liberation from a stillness to a movement, a rise; protests happen with a walk, nations have gained their independence with the walk, emperors ousted, dictators overthrown by the march of the crowds; every life shows movement in as much as it is capable of, from itself, by itself, within itself, which is something of a walk; there is no external stimuli to walk—just get up and walk so your thoughts can run, give your legs a chance so your mind can speak, so it can do what it must, which is to think—isn't it what it's meant to do? A life of little thought is a life lived vain and dry; for even the lowest of all animals do what nature wishes—a primitive walk—the basic form of action and movement.

§

The dark clouds draw a curtain over a beautiful landscape on my imagination; the sun is lost somewhere in those clouds, not seen, yet I see light, like his remains in them, just as there is light on a starry night; nonetheless it may happen that a clear night sky never gives in, the heavens refuse to open up, for a peek, but if that is so, so be it, there is still the moon to see, to hope, to study, full or part, bright or blurry, a sliver each day, till he will also disappear, vanish for a time, for us to reflect; so is life—there will be a time when the dark is truly a dark, a night fully a night, when darkness pervades all around, so much so that even a dim candlelight grants a much needed respite—who would have thought and who would have known?—I say Fate. Can we conquer Fate? Understand it? We must, we have to, and we already do, in our every attempt, in every strife, in every suffering, in every triumph, in every jubilation, for what is human progress other than this, a valiant, ambitious, and laudable quest of understanding Fate?

§

The golden rays penetrate through the sky; suddenly a dull cloud cover appears radiant, turning the gray into a gold, like alchemy but real; a golden hope lives in this heavenly spectacle—this is the work of the setting sun, a treat the sun affords to each one of us as the day ends, perhaps to dwell on a much needed hope in the darkness of the night.

§

Winter arrives, days become shorter, the sun feels cooler, less bright; the road is the same but my walk feels a little different—a bother; it is not the cold nor the short day that I can say is the source of this amiss, but something else, something gloomy that lives in the air; the dry leaves, the withering trees, the freezing windchill attest my thoughts; granted there is beauty in each of these but today I can't see any; my heart feels a little heavy, my head a little distraught, I doubt any amount of wealth can buy me some enthusiasm—perhaps the reason I think of the many festivals celebrated on the onset or the heart of every winter, in the east or the west; it's not the triumph of good over evil or the birth of a messiah. It's just man's fight against nature's will, for a sense, for a longing, for a belonging, for a community, to fight the gloom, to fight the dark that pervades through and through in the silence of the night.

§

The walk in the woods is really a walk of our minds. With every step we give ourselves a chance to see nature's work and in each step lies a voice; I say listen as if it were our own, it speaks as clearly as nature shows—the colors of our heart and the dreams of our mind.

§

This heart is one; it works alone; nourishes, nurtures every organ this body has yet it asks nothing in return; it's as if nature's essence is condensed and crystallized in this organ—the size of a fist—whose grip holds the pulse, the breath of life. How mighty it is for the size that it *is*, how selfless it remains for the power that it *has*, and how noble it becomes for what it *does*; quite rightfully the heart is the organ that announces the beginning of life with its first beat and signals the end with its last; even the head, the seat of reason, of intellect, readily yields and bows to the heart when the heart speaks, for this heart guards life like a star—the first to live and the last to die.

§

Fate smiles and Life fights. Life has in her arsenal hope and inspiration, will and determination, to play a game with Fate, one which Fate demands, right from her bare beginnings to her robed end. Fate, the lord and master of one and all, pervades throughout and never ceases his grip on the course of this world. This game where what is given today may be taken back tomorrow, where we have a choice yet from a governed set, is a never-ending affair, like a possession we have but for how long we do not know. And so as we put on many hats in this world so we can find joy and happiness, wealth and fame, it becomes clear to us that in the end we remain governed by the rules of cause and effect—Fate's kingpins—in this life we live. It is Fate that sets the course and it is Fate that gives us the script we are to follow. So, in the end, even if Fate has reduced us to mere actors in his treacherous plot, Life through her will forces us to strive so we can leave a mark in Fate's grand book, and for this fight our Life stands up to, in spite of knowing how she will end, for her valor, what we must do is to look Fate in the eye . . . and smile back.

INTRODUCTION TO CHAPTER 3

Art lives in every human invention. But it speaks vividly in a poem, an essay, a painting, or a musical composition. Every other form of invention is rendered secondary, the primary stands out, which is what art invariably reflects—truth. We can attest confidently the following statement—where art ends, science begins. Without the former to reflect, the latter would not repeat. I have no hesitation in saying that this world, this universe is a work of art, for even in its randomness, there is an order, in the darkness is seen a spark—the brightness of a star. In this chapter, I highlight the fine arts of poetry, music, painting, and literature, with perhaps a special affinity to that of music. Music—for me is special—not just for enjoyment but for discovery. With nothing more to say, I leave you in the company of these lines—they belong to the arts . . . music in particular.

CHAPTER 3

On Arts

A pianist brings to life the nuances in a musical composition; the slurs, the lifts, the rests, the staccatos, the legatos give a completely different meaning to a song, a whole new dimension to a melody; it transforms a pleasant piece into a majestic show; the fingers, the hands, come together in unison to bring about this transformation—how lovely the music sounds and how grand the pianist looks when he plays the piece in its entirety, with the technique, with emotion, with devotion, like the composer himself; the art of playing the piano or for that matter any musical instrument is much, much more than a recital of the original score; it's a submission, of the heart and the soul, seen in the act, with the posture, in the movement of the hands, the dance of the fingers, a salute I say, to the unyielding power of music.

§

Music must hold a higher place in all the fields of knowledge; this is perhaps beautifully highlighted when we are in the company of a child who is in his first year, on how he moves, smiles, or waves when a tone falls on his ears; or when he has to be pacified to sleep, comforted in our arms, it is music that comes to the rescue; in its melody he finds a comfort; and from its language he derives a speech, like he knows the grammar, follows the text, thus showing each and every one of us the reach and range of this fine art of music. Music illustrates from a distance what life remains at its core, on how it feels to live a circumstance without actually living it—even science for all its might lags behind, for science enumerates a method to unravel the truth . . . but music . . . I say . . . it goes even further—it has the means to discover the truth itself—be it the subjective passions in our hearts or the objective reasons of this world.

§

A picture celebrates individuality, a verse highlights the commonality, and music expresses the universality—the indulgence in each of them has its own reward—a comfort that is privy to the heart alone, one that is its true wealth and remains its only need.

§

Every meaningful verse lightens the mood in the quiet of the night; even a worry dampens in the melody therein; such is the effect . . . everything great in poetry brings a meaning to this two-faced life, be it night or day—poetry mends the rift, while music bridges the gulf, lending the verse its notes, thus making the verse even more instructive and readily acceptable; in effect we see something spectacular, a glorious attempt to weave a flash of human thought—a verse—into the language of the heavens—music.

§

There lies a universal philosophy behind every great verse; in essence such a verse opens a whole new world for us, a world we neglect and forgo as we live, yet one that lives inside us quietly and patiently. This is a world of ideas, a world that waits to be awakened and comes to life with the aid of instruction or by the hand of experience. Every great discovery or a monumental achievement confirms this fact, when an inborn necessity speaks, or the inward eye shows what every great verse says—revealing a world of infinite and eternal ideas for our curious minds to see.

§

Every episode in life seems to have an ally in music. It's as if the tunes and harmony accorded to music exist to comfort us so we can live and feel its essence while we enjoy the melody of a piece. Music speaks to us with such profundity yet with such simplicity that we can relate to the ideas therein, moving us from the specifics to the general, the present to the perceptual, the real to the ideal, thus forging a bond with those who have *borne* and with those who have *felt*. This universal art of action and movement with its meter and melody reminds us that at the bottom we remain one and the same, made of the same material, born from the same spirit, whose force many a time we proudly admire and at other times shamefully lament. Yet in spite of such an objective and a detached picture of oneness, music remains deeply personal, offering a chance for every life to escape from itself, from the dull and dreary affairs of this world to a world of its own—a world of ideas—elevating, uplifting, consoling, and even a steady one.

§

A musical composition does not aim to highlight the prose of a single life, which is different for every man, woman, or child, but seeks to narrate the poetry therein, that remains the same for everyone, follows a similar theme, and holds true to its word in every culture, in every land, and even perhaps in every life. The idea of life, the numerous shades of her happiness, her sadness, her pain, her suffering, her craving, or even her excitement can be written down within a measure in a musical composition; these notes and measures reveal to us the depth of our inner nature, something that no man can do, for music in itself *has* an innate purity that no man fully *has,* and *is* a paragon of godliness that no man really *is*.

§

A musical melody can be imperfect, even coarse, it may require ample polish to soothe the ear, or perfect the tune, but it is never erroneous in itself; this demonstrates the class of music, which for all the universality it brings to our world remains a language that allows us to express our own individuality; we are truly our own in the company of music, we live in the world yet are allowed to be absent from it; such is the depth of music as well its breadth, all of which we fully grasp from our beginning till our very end—a reliable companion of our life.

§

Music stands apart from every other field of art or science: it offers a continuous source of relaxation and enjoyment, which each of us can always count on, come home to; every encounter with our favorite piece is new in itself, like meeting a beloved friend, or a near and dear one, the melody offers a fresh look, a different view and sometimes even a consolation after every recital; we might as well say that music helps us see life and her many shades as they are—detached but still felt—as opposed to those that get muddled with our experiences—attached and hence felt—when we live our life in the actual.

§

The story of our life is perhaps a mathematical equation and simultaneously a musical melody; all the emotions are in the melody therein and the consequents the result of the equation thereof. Music is a language the world fully grasps; beneath the handful notes of music is a mystery mathematics strives to prove.

§

A musical composition is brought to life by the artist who plays it. The notes and rests have to be played exactly, as represented, even a minor miss can disturb the overall effect. Music answers what our feelings ask and the bridge that makes this happen is the composition itself. There are no second chances in a musical performance, as what is felt is directly affected by continuity of the melody. Any disturbance to the sequence can spoil the tone and sometimes even our mood. For this the artist bears great responsibility, as he must attempt to play the piece in the same vein the composer had felt. Every heartfelt performance highlights the goal of a musical composition; it aspires to win our hearts rather than rule our heads—a sign of honest intentions, high aims, and a hallmark of genuine work.

§

Life begins with the first beat of heart and ends with its last one. The heart strives with its will alone all that it sets out to do—holding the pulse of life itself. Weak or strong, one or many, day or night, it does what it must, neither resting nor ceasing, being the center, the source of nourishment for every limb and spine the body has. Such is the life of the heart, it beats so others can live, just like a star, *the first to live and the last to die.* The rhythms of the heart find an ally in music, as music speaks the language that the heart wishes to hear, of beat and rest; a pure, clean text of life herself in her most nimble and raw form. Melody is a direct friend of the heart, so they say, and why not, for both of them understand each other—thoroughly and deeply. How apt it is that for all matters the heart deems close to itself, the heart rules, for as rightly said, the heart has reasons that it only knows of.

§

An orchestra symbolizes the idea of life quite splendidly and majestically. In that hour of symphony, every acoustic in the group supplies the melody at the right time and for a precise duration so that the overall rhythm and rhyme of the song are left intact. They work in unison, sometimes loud and other times fade, a harmony of the tune as well as the tone, thereby preserving the essence of that masterpiece.

As far as the orchestra can carry, it remains at the mercy of the conductor, who is the center, the guide, the guardian, and the sole master who decides when every piece can have its time and its turn. No matter how grand any piece is, when its turn ends, it too goes silent until called again. Life is also like that, with every episode written in it, when it begins so shall it end, leaving the stage open for the next to follow. So, every moment that has now gone, becomes an experience on which life looks forward to her next ask. The unseen master, the conductor, guides her to the next stanza, that deterministic force, or more generally the hand of fate, to whom we owe the pieces of our life's musical.

§

The star-studded world we live in, which remains hidden to our eye in the light of the day opens up only in the dark of the night; the specks of stars that light up the sky are a spectacle to watch, and even if we know nothing about what we see, their inner details so to speak, they hold our gaze as if we are in search for something, a subconscious drive, to fulfill not just the want of our mind but the need of our heart. These thousand lights adorn the sky, like jewels, in their precise constellations, obeying a pattern, circling their masters, the suns. They are a well-laid-out arrangement that only an artist could have thought of, for how else are we to explain the beauty and magnificence behind it, it must be something more than human reason can *reason*, an artist's will perhaps, which may be beyond our capacity to apprehend or reason; reason may help understand, but such a responsibility is in the hands of art, art alone. Even pure mathematics, the bedrock on which all of natural sciences rest, ends up as an art of symbols—to those who live for and breathe in it, for they guard it, defend it like a prized possession, a work of art, thus highlighting the innateness of art, rightly called—a mirror of truth.

§

Music grants every feeling of adventure a place to rest and a chance to be reborn; our feelings that arise from all our strivings are common across our species, they find the ear of our companions whether to their strife or their relief, we celebrate momentous victories and share heartbreaking losses with our fellowmen, our near and dear, our kin; but once all this merriment and excitement is over, and when life shows her true color, on how lonely and repetitive she can be, music comes along, reminding us of that endeavor, which we can relive for a brief time from our past and end with a hope for our future.

§

How music can move us so much without much ado is perhaps a mystery that has a deeper answer than what we can reason. It is the only subject that we fully comprehend in our depths without ever a need of a study and is one that remains unmatched not just in style but in stature as well. Every meaningful note our heart gets accustomed to never leaves our head, it resonates with the idea within us, speaking about itself, showing us the reach of this exceedingly fine art of music.

§

There must be a world more beautiful than the one we live in, a world where we long to be, a world untouched and unspoiled by the footprints of any man—essentially one that we can see, think, or feel yet have never laid our feet on to call it our own. A beautiful sunset, a heartfelt verse, or a penetrating melody, which each of us can see, think or feel but can never alter or spoil, perhaps reflects this fact—there lies a place far richer than our own and remains well beyond the influence of our will and command. Art outlines such a world by its painting, Poetry renders it through its verses, while Music subsumes it by its melody, and how rightly so, for these three illustrious fields do what others cannot, they live and exist to serve what they truly represent—the ideas themselves.

§

It is remarkable and perhaps even satisfying that every great verse speaks in its own way the essence of the idea therein. The immediate comprehension of what the verse speaks of is as natural as breathing, hardly is there a need of conscious thinking, everything is evident as it should be, as it must, and from here we can see why such a work is a hallmark of genius—for it discovers for us what we always look for but what we never really see.

§

Music takes a long time to master; a skillful musician works for years to learn and perfect his art; it's as if perfection is a necessity to highlight the essence of what we innately know, life and living thereof, the greatness being that all this happens in just one sitting whenever the artist plays the piece. Every tune in itself has a distinct message and speaks of the prevailing nature of life; even science with its admirable quest to understand life, her many subtleties, cannot match the universality and depth that music has, as science demands a certain knowledge, the understanding of the many relations, the various symbols, and the burden of a thousand complexities that come with its study, thus limiting its audience only to a select few. But music, it imposes no such demand, all it seeks is a willing heart, to whom it speaks in the most penetrating tone the crux of the matter, of what life really is, *not how she works but how she is*, the many shades of her happiness, her sadness, her pain, her suffering, her craving, and so on, essentially a truth we need not learn but one we fully grasp in all our flesh and blood.

§

Music speaks the language of life. In its most bare form, a musical sequence is written as a measure, a string of notes interleaved with a beat and a rest. These notations are plain symbols but how powerful are they, for in this simple draw, lies the wonder and magic of the rich and illustrious art of music. And once these notes come to life from the hands of a gifted artist, we see their power—from a simple grammar originates a common and a universal language, a language we need not learn yet whose text we fully follow, one whose vocabulary is etched in each of us innately and minutely, all in all a language of life herself. In every heartfelt musical encounter is felt a pulse of life flowing through, as the head yields and the heart wills to enjoy the show of emotions brought to light by the composition itself. The heart is the first to feel such a penetrating effect, and how rightly so, for the heart is the organ that does the same; it plays a musical sequence, of a beat and a rest, a simple yet a full measure in itself, and one without its first beat, life would never have begun. Music is an art of such class and distinction that no head can claim to fully describe its greatness, since the heart does this job by playing the tune of life—the rhythm of beat and rest—day after day, night after night in the many forms that live or thrive.

§

The goodness of children and the godliness of music align in character and resonate in spirit, and are perhaps why this fine art of music comes to a willing child with such ease and flow as if it is one of their own.

§

In the evergreen compositions of the musicians, life's character has been revealed, which time and again has preserved its texture, one that has not changed a thousand years since and one that will not change a thousand years hence.

§

The heart wins over the head when it finds a melody it can tune itself to; it's as if the heart now runs the show while the head rests listening to all that the heart has to say—when there is music the head need not look, since the heart finds what it wants, a mate, a friend who converses in a language it only knows of—beat and rest.

§

The joys, the sorrows, the sufferings, the misfortunes, the disappointments, and the strivings that each of us live in the actual world are spoken by music in the abstract.

§

Poetry is a subject that brings out the idea in a simple form; in a few lines it accomplishes what prose takes a many, it remains a human invention, essentially a product of human imagination, showing the power and reach of human thought, accessible to one and all, the only bind being the language it uses to say all that everyone feels, perhaps an art weaved with reason, one that conveys the depth as well as the vastness, essentially the essence, of the idea itself.

§

Poetry is a subject that can befriend the reason of Philosophy and the melody of Music. How easily it blends into each one is remarkable; it is perhaps the only subject known to man that bridges the two effortlessly and ceaselessly, the verses carry a deeper philosophical meaning yet they can adapt to the language of music; in here a man needs no formal or a progressive study to contribute to the vast and varied repertoire; it comes to him because it must, is an expression of life herself, of her inner nature, her texture, and sometimes even her workings, that each of us lives with and hence each of us fully grasps.

§

Poetry has a lot more in common with Music than what we see; every new composition stands on its own merit, their makers work alone, seldom do they need anyone else as their imagination supplies them their inspiration, and even if what they do is wholly the product of their own thinking, they end up saying what has been said a thousand times before and what will be said a thousand times again, but with their own unique touch, a fresh look, that makes their work full of class and distinction. Poetry may lose its voice in the noise of this world, but it is poetry that makes us see what we fail to look for in the rabble of life. Poetry is the only subject that can come close to accompany Music in its work, because just like Music, a poem speaks in its own way of what is true and what remains immortal—the idea itself.

§

It is a characteristic of a great poem to illustrate in a clear and convincing manner the idea it speaks of; the poet conveys all what he wishes to say by the use of words alone, neither his rank nor his title can have any influence on the final impression it leaves on the reader. Every new composition starts from a naught, a new beginning, as the fresh ink fills up the blank paper with only imagination as the real company. Poetry is a subject that can never be taught, it comes to those by its own will and command. It allows them to say what they see and think of all that others have spoken, yet in their own distinct and unique manner, one that makes it their own, akin to life, which follows the same course in every land but remains distinct and unique in the eyes of each one.

§

Some of the finest compositions in music are enjoyed only when we are alone, in solitude. Even in the setting of an orchestra where there is an audience, we can see this happening, how the melody unites everyone in spirit yet offers each one full freedom to be engrossed in the music thoroughly and completely. The tunes and tones born from this rich and wonderful art of music lifts us out from all the petty affairs of this world to an elevated state, one that we may never get to be in because this world says so, but one that we are at least granted to feel for a time, albeit short, while the melody plays out that piece.

§

How striking it is that verses and melodies through the medium of print preserve their content while every other form of art, be it weaving, sculpture, painting, architecture, cannot do so in spite of how beautiful they look—time fades away their color or distorts their shape. While both are praiseworthy only one of them lives long—only one weaves the ideas in abstract while the other does so in actual.

§

Every writer has a style of his own, be it in prose or poetry. While the style shows in the writer's work till its finish, what ends up leaving the mark are the ideas that his words speak of. So those words that live long to be read and recited for generations and generations are really the means to reflect on the idea itself, a condition, a necessity of all life and the living that goes with it. And how apt is this arrangement that even if every life has to end, her words get to live as they exist only to serve those ideas that they truly represent.

§

A pensive moment brings with it a brush of hope and a shade of inspiration. A verse, a tune, or a thought possessing such a quality does this job quite well, for even a tear when it dries up leaves a mark and has the power for the head to reflect and the heart to hope.

§

Thoughts of the poetic and the musical seldom age as they are the bridge between the abstract and the actual. Every other beautiful source somehow falls to time, yet here they are, living in a realm of their own, having a timeless appeal of permanence like the ideas themselves—the nerve and the fiber of this whole world.

§

Music and Poetry are the means to peek into our inner nature. They are reflective and remain by our side like a caring hand, as they speak to our being, connecting the dots and telling us that howsoever different we may appear on our faces, how similar we remain in our hearts. Hence in times of confusion, commotion, whirl, turmoil, doubt, distress, cheer, glory, these two aides come to the rescue, like comrades do to each other. There is a hint of worldly wisdom in a poetic verse, and an element of truth in every musical tone that each of us submits to and silently obeys, suggesting that both these illustrious fields are meant for the discovery of truth—be it the passions of the heart or the reasons of the head.

§

All of the esteemed fields of art have one thing in common—they come to life in the setting of silence and solitude. A painter's brush, a writer's pen, or a musician's notes need no company; mere tools they are ... yet they have the powers to win hearts and through them every gifted artist can show the world the power of individuality. They illustrate in the clearest of terms that at the bottom every work of art, a verse, a melody, or a painting remains the work of only a single mind meant to nourish the individual first and then through him his species.

§

Life has in her book two elements, one of prose and the other of poetry. The prose is the detail, or the chapters as such, whereas poetry condenses the meaning in them. Quite naturally we see this happening, all our past, from our joys to our sorrows, when called by the mind, how easily is the meaning comprehended in summary, as how poetry reaches the depth in just a few lines. Poetry shows life's similarity and prose her distinction.

§

It is in the melody of music that words find a way out to express the meaning of the tone and the tune. Almost many a time there is a loss in translation, but every word that comes out from such a reliable aide, whence one's feeling finds her freedom, ends up speaking volumes of life's inner nature, showing the individuality of one's thought yet the similarity of a common truth.

§

Words are the remains of a human life, which must end in due course. They are the objects of our thoughts and are our own very unique structures of what we feel, what we wish in the flow of our life; thereby surpassing all the actions that any life goes through. For every past action is a summary of an episode, but words can be the synopsis of that life. They have the might to live for centuries, perhaps eternity if preserved, like music they bring warmth to our souls with their wit and wisdom. Actions may be remembered for what they are but we cannot relive them, actions remain frozen; actions are at the mercy of time, but words, they go far, and if said from the lips or the pen of a right mind, they show their powers, their reach and are the live footprints of the mind that borne them.

§

For every melody, there is an ear—happens to be a principle of a universal nature. Poetry finds a reliable ally in melody like a friend is to other. While both are illustrious and rule in their own league, when weaved together and done right, the effect is like the meet of the glorious, the verse flows with ease and flair unlocking and unwrapping the meaning as the melody supplying the base on which the verse lives. Melody can uplift an ordinary verse thereby making the mood, but the same cannot be said of the inverse.

§

Worthy thoughts resemble the comets that come and go; the comets cannot be summoned every so often as their allegiance is to a sole master—the sun—to whom they owe their range and also their orbit. And even the sun obliges and waits his turn to witness their arrival when called upon—such is the length of their journey round the world. Likewise, a lofty thought, a novel idea, or for that matter even the right word, an original so to speak, resembles a comet, as such thoughts obey a different master and arrive quite suddenly when least expected, like the comets we see.

§

In the field of theatre is found the final expressions that a generation wishes and longs for. How mighty is the power of the pen is visible here, a scene that we never experience can be felt by us, as if someone else is conveying their wants that we unknowingly desire. The closest way to experience such a thing is through a story from which we are detached but yet bound by what all of us enlist and all of us endure—our feelings.

§

Living is life, a writer's material, an artist's pulse, a composer's measure. This God-given life has its walks and turns, every life has many, perhaps far too many to speak, unique in themselves, never losing an identify of themselves. It is astonishing and even refreshing to see life birthing to a form from a rock, a stardust so to speak, in effect galaxies have come together to make this moment, make me happen, to make my life as well as yours. So I wonder sometimes, if we are to condense every moment of my life and join them to yours and the countless others, and create a manuscript, what would this look like—will it be repetitive, but bewildering, original but dull—like a task, a job—a day in the life of a star? There is no escape, we are in the end one, one culture, one race, one species, which looks up to the heavens to find our truths, in the hymns or the symbols, in science or art, and while each of us lives our life to the tune of our own breaths, we live so to speak for a posterity, for an advance, a betterment, or a beginning, just as the hand or the rock who made me a me, and one who made you a you.

§

The thought itself is laden with instinct, impulse, and initiation. It needs no language to live, how wonderful and free a thought is, in the confines of a higher plane, the safety of the mind; language gives expression to a thought; a gifted writer uses language to dress it up majestically for the world to savor and enjoy while preserving the sanctity of what it represents. Every beautiful expression rests on the thought itself, the weight, substance, and its force—language is simply the means to convey its composition—the essence itself.

About the Author

AMEYA DILIP PANDIT is an engineer by trade. His work spans across all the layers of a complex software system. While his profession deals with the physical aspects of the world, his writings strive to investigate the finer aspects of life. His journal is his escape, the remains of which he compiles from time to time into a more condensed essay, a poem, a letter, for any record as such.

For him art remains a source of truth, and science the means to understand it.

He lives in Southern California with his wife and their two children.

Visit his website at panditletters.com

www.ingramcontent.com/pod-product-compliance
Lightning Source LLC
Chambersburg PA
CBHW020910080526

44589CB00011B/531